Unrespectable Verse

EDITED BY

GEOFFREY GRIGSON

ALLEN LANE THE PENGUIN PRESS

Introduction and selection copyright © Geoffrey Grigson, 1971

First published in 1971

Allen Lane The Penguin Press
Vigo Street, London W1

ISBN 0 7139 0241 8

Printed in Great Britain by
Richard Clay (The Chaucer Press) Ltd
Bungay, Suffolk
Set in Monotype Bembo

To the memory of Norman Cameron

Contents

Acknowledgements

For permission to reprint poems in copyright, thanks are due to the following:

W. H. AUDEN: an extract from 'Marginalia' from *City Without Walls*, 1969, 'Postscript to the Prologue' from *About the House*, 1966, and 'Academic Graffiti' from *Homage to Clio*, 1960, to Faber & Faber Ltd.

MAX BEERBOHM: from *Max in Verse*, 1964, to Max Beerbohm, J. G. Riewald, William Heinemann Ltd, and the Stephen Greene Press.

HILAIRE BELLOC: 'Aunt Jane' from *Cautionary Verses*, 1940, to Gerald Duckworth & Co. Ltd; 'Justice of the Peace', 'On Mundane Acquaintances' and 'On a Puritan' from *Complete Verses*, 1940, published by Gerald Duckworth & Co. Ltd, to A. D. Peters & Co.

NORMAN CAMERON: 'A Visit to the Dead', 'Public House Confidence', 'Punishment Enough' and 'Lucifer' from *Collected Poems 1905–53*, published 1967 by the Hogarth Press, and translations of Arthur Rimbaud, from *Selected Poems of Arthur Rimbaud*, 1942, to Alan S. Hodge and the Hogarth Press; for 'Ballade' from *The Selected Poems of François Villon*, 1952, translated by Norman Cameron, by permission of Alan S. Hodge and Jonathan Cape Ltd.

ROY CAMPBELL: 'A Veld Eclogue: The Pioneers' from *Nativity*, 1954, published by Faber & Faber Ltd, to the Estate of Roy Campbell; for translations from Baudelaire from *Les Fleurs du mal*, published by Harvill Press, to Hughes Massie Ltd.

C. P. CAVAFY: from *Collected Poems*, 1961, to the translator Rae Dalven, and the Hogarth Press.

ROBERT CREELEY: from *The Finger*, 1970, to Calder & Boyars Ltd.

E. E. CUMMINGS: from *Complete Poems of E. E. Cummings*, 1968, to MacGibbon & Kee Ltd.

DAFYDD AP GWILYM: from *Twenty-Five Poems of Dafydd ap Gwilym*, translated by Nigel Heseltine, 1968, the Piers Press, to A. D. Peters & Co.

W. H. DAVIES: from *The Complete Poems of W. H. Davies*, 1963, to Mrs H. M. Davies and Jonathan Cape Ltd.

WALTER DE LA MARE: from *Complete Poems of Walter de la Mare*, 1969, Faber & Faber Ltd, to the Literary Trustees of Walter de la Mare and the Society of Authors as their representative.

T. S. ELIOT: from *Collected Poems 1909–1962*, 1963, to Faber & Faber Ltd.

LAWRENCE FERLINGHETTI: translations from Jacques Prévert from *Selections from Paroles*, copyright © 1947 by Les Editions du Point du Jour, Paris. Reprinted by permission of City Lights Books, San Francisco.

ALLEN GINSBERG: from *Howl and Other Poems*, copyright © 1956, 1959, by Allen Ginsberg. Reprinted by permission of City Lights Books, San Francisco.

LEWIS GLYN COTHI: from *A Celtic Miscellany*, 1951, Routledge & Kegan Paul, to the translator, Kenneth Hurlstone Jackson. This version is taken from the Penguin edition of *A Celtic Miscellany*, 1971.

OLIVER ST JOHN GOGARTY: 'The Hay Hotel' and 'On First Looking into Krafft-Ebing's *Psychopathia Sexualis*' from *Oliver St John Gogarty*, 1964, edited by U. O'Connor and published by Jonathan Cape Ltd, to Oliver D. Gogarty; 'Ringsend' and 'Elegy on the Archpoet William Butler Yeats', from *Collected Poems*, 1951, to Constable & Co. Ltd.

HARRY GRAHAM: from *Ruthless Rhymes for Heartless Homes*, 1901, to Edward Arnold (Publishers) Ltd.

ROBERT GRAVES: 'In Committee' from *Collected Poems 1914–1927*, 'The Enlisted Man' from *Collected Poems*, 1959, and 'To Evoke Posterity', 'The Laureate', 'Down, Wanton, Down', 'The Thieves' and 'A Royal Duke (from Grotesques)' from *Collected Poems*, 1965, to Cassell & Co. Ltd and Robert Graves.

GEOFFREY GRIGSON: to the author.

THOMAS HARDY: from *Collected Poems of Thomas Hardy*, 1930, reprinted by permission of the Trustees of the Hardy Estate and Macmillan & Co. Ltd.

A. D. HOPE: from *Collected Poems*, by A. D. Hope, copyright © 1961, to Hamish Hamilton, London.

A. E. HOUSMAN: from *Complete Poems*, 1967, to the Society of Authors as the literary representative of the Estate of A. E. Housman, and to Jonathan Cape Ltd.

PHILIP LARKIN: from *The Whitsun Weddings*, 1964, to Faber & Faber Ltd.

D. H. LAWRENCE: from *Complete Poems*, 1964, William Heinemann Ltd, to Laurence Pollinger Ltd and the Estate of the late Mrs Frieda Lawrence.

WYNDHAM LEWIS: from *One Way Song*, 1960, to Methuen & Co. Ltd.

PHYLLIS MCGINLEY: from *The Love Letters of Phyllis McGinley*, 1955, to Secker & Warburg Ltd and Phyllis McGinley.

LOUIS MACNEICE: from *The Collected Poems of Louis MacNeice*, 1966, to Faber & Faber Ltd.

EDGAR LEE MASTERS: from *The Spoon River Anthology*, 1962, Collier-Macmillan Ltd, to Weissberger & Frosch, New York, on behalf of Mrs Edgar Lee Masters.

ADRIAN MITCHELL: 'Fifteen Million Plastic Bags', 'If I had a Concrete Mixer', 'Quite Apart from the Holy Ghost', 'Another Prince is Born' and 'Riddle' from *Poems*, 1964, to Adrian Mitchell and Jonathan Cape Ltd; 'To Whom it May Concern', 'Celia, Celia' and 'Adrian Mitchell's Famous Weak Bladder Blues' from *Out Loud*, 1968, to Adrian Mitchell and Cape Goliard. (*Out Loud* is distributed in the United States by Grossman Publishers Inc.)

MARIANNE MOORE: from *The Complete Poems of Marianne Moore*, 1968, to Faber & Faber Ltd.

WILFRED OWEN: from *Collected Poems*, 1963, to Mr Harold Owen and Chatto & Windus Ltd.

SIR WALTER RALEIGH: from *Laughter from a Cloud*, 1923, to Constable & Co. Ltd.

JOHN CROWE RANSOM: from *Selected Poems*, 1948, Eyre & Spottiswoode Ltd, to the Proprietors, Alfred A. Knopf/Random House Inc., and Lawrence Pollinger Ltd.

EDGELL RICKWORD: from *Fifty Poems*, Enitharmon Press, to the author.

EDWIN ARLINGTON ROBINSON: 'Miniver Cheevy' (copyright 1907 Charles Scribner's Sons; renewal copyright 1935) is reprinted by permission of Charles Scribner's Sons from *The Town Down the River* by Edwin Arlington Robinson.

SIEGFRIED SASSOON: from *Collected Poems 1908–56*, 1961, Faber & Faber Ltd, to G. T. Sassoon.

STEVIE SMITH: from *The Frog Prince and Other Poems*, 1966, to Longman Group Ltd.

GEORGE STARBUCK: Reprinted with permission from *The New York Review of Books*. Copyright © 1970 NYREV Inc.

ACKNOWLEDGEMENTS

JAMES STEPHENS: from *Collected Poems of James Stephens*, 1954, to Mrs Iris Wise and Macmillan & Co. Ltd.

HUMBERT WOLFE: to Ann Wolfe.

W. B. YEATS: from *Collected Poems of W. B. Yeats*, 1950, to M. B. Yeats and Macmillan & Co. Ltd.

Every effort has been made to trace copyright holders, but in a few cases this has proved impossible. The publishers would be interested to hear from any copyright holders not here acknowledged.

Introduction

Isn't art subversive? To be sure of the right answer, one would
have to know what is being subverted: one would have to
clothe oneself, for a moment, in the attitudes of mind habitual
to a Minister for Home Affairs. 'Subversive' is a word used by
those who defend the perfection or at any rate the desirability
of things, not as they are, but as they ought to be according to
respectable opinion, according to what is held to be a suffi-
ciently large or important consensus; consensus being an older
term for what we have come to personalize as an Establish-
ment, or as *the* Establishment.

Subversion is censorious or bloody-minded.

It may wish to correct, to adjust, at any rate to affirm rather
than overthrow – 'the thin end of the wedge' as an Attorney-
General with a weak case might say in the courts.

Defenders against subversion are in arms, sometimes literally
and offensively, to maintain 'our inheritance': we inherit a
God, and taboos and moral virtues, notions of man and
family, and constitutional practices, shibboleths of theocracy
and law; we inherit, as well as the old arrangements which
'work', the revolutions which have succeeded; and defenders
include not only the respectable for whom such words are
found as 'the Silent Majority', but the various professional
militia of society, the specialists – judges, priests, generals,
colonels, police (who always tend to become 'secret' police),
'intelligence' bureaux, bureaucrats, educators, editors, literary
critics.

If one took the conspiratorial view of social man, or the
views, say, of many who attack 'the Establishment', society
would be divided rigidly into defenders of every kind and

subverters of every kind; and these with equal rigidity would be subdivided into categories altogether excluding other categories. Luckily the true condition of most of us is mixed; is grey, rather even than piebald. We each of us, even the reactionaries and the revolutionaries, to some degree defend, to some degree subvert; and as a result societies hold – with a special debt to the critical subversion exercised by artists, and especially the artists of literature. There is plenty in all respectable settled life to stoke their risibility or exasperation, or more extremely, their hatred and contempt.

So I come to my class in poetry, in poems (rather than poets) of the 'unrespectable'. The poets, of course, are each of them mixed, even if this time piebald, or coloured by a bright concatenation of colours and emotional attitudes, rather than grey; few genuine poets writing either 'respectably' or 'unrespectably' all the time. There are – but I see that I shall still have to explain my chosen adjective and its opposite more clearly – quite strong elements of the unrespectable in, let us say, Kipling or Eliot; of the respectable in Villon, or in those most wonderful, and wonderfully diverse masters of the unrespectable, Rochester and William Blake.

A word rears up which I must dispose of straight away. Satire. This is no collection by and large, or exclusively, from the satirists. I have drawn rather little on the classic familiarities of satire; which is respectable rather than unrespectable. There are exceptions, I agree, but the poet in his role – if at any rate it is his dominant role – as satirist condemns with exceptional vigour what a respectable consensus also condemns: he is its mouthpiece, as conservative as any. When I thought of this anthology, I intended to include a now rather neglected, though once famous piece which lies between poetry and prose. This was the mock epitaph on Francis Charteris, which was written by John Arbuthnot, the friend of Swift and Pope, and fellow member of the Scriblerus Club:

Here continueth to rot
The body of FRANCIS CHARTERIS,
Who, with an Inflexible Constancy
and
Inimitable Uniformity of Life
Persisted
In spite of *Age* and *Infirmities*
In the practice of *Every Human Vice*
Excepting *Prodigality* and *Hypocrisy*:
His insatiable *Avarice* exempted him from the first
His matchless *Impudence* from the second . . .

– and so on, in wit which is certainly scathing and strong. But then looking through it again, of course I realized it was respectable rather than unrespectable: what could anyone do except condemn this Colonel Charteris, who was universally known to be a cheat, a thief, a gambler, a con-man, a bully, a procurer, a rapist?

Out with that, in consequence; but in with a good many pieces of witty exasperation – now we are nearer the centre of this particular concern – pieces, for example, by Alexander Pope,

Cibber! write all thy Verses upon Glasses,
The only way to save 'em from our Arses,

who was predominantly *poet*, with very exceptional reasons, of physique and fate and personality, for exasperated laughter, rather than *satirist*, let us say, in the way of John Dryden. At least it seems to me that rubicund and bland Dryden writes from an exceptionally conforming genius; if one looks in him or in his verse for a person, one finds, rather, something greatly and smoothly vertical or horizontal, a kind of shape or figure. But the case is a little different when for once this great Dryden is personally exasperated; for example, by a mean response from his publisher, whereupon – if the tradition is true – he

sends back the messenger with that triplet of excellently funny
lines, which I do include, and properly so,

> With leering Looks, Bullfac'd, and freckl'd fair,
> With two left Legs, and *Judas*-colour'd Hair
> And frowzy Pores that taint the ambient Air,

accompanied by threats of worse to follow. The respectable
way to write to one's publisher is of course different; there are
always provident ways of altering one's first typewritten draft.

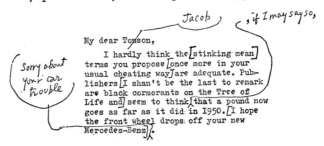

Etcetera. I wish, by the way, I could have found more poems
about publishers, towards whom (I think) authors are now-
adays not quite as honest in the expression of their sentiments
as they would like to be.

Of course, I am not arguing that one can always exactly
distinguish between satire, from the base of consensus and im-
personality, and the unrespectable verse which arises out of
strong personal exasperation; and I am far from pretending
that everything in my choice maintains a flawless consistency
of motive and attitude. I incline, though, in every one of my
ten sections, to the personally wry, the personally unrespect-
able, or subversive; in which the elements of unrespectability
may be far from identical.

Separate or combined, the poem may afford unrespect-
ability of manner, unrespectability of language, unrespect-
ability of concern. It may be concerned with something which

a respectable, sufficiently numerous or influential consensus
avoids, such as the foolishness of the Lord's anointed or the
improbability of the Lord who anoints. Marvell, Restoration
or no, designates Charles II for all time as the Priapus King
(p. 31), Max Beerbohm (p. 30) tries to decide between the
degrees of dullness which were evident in George V and
Queen Mary –

> Lady, you lie. Last evening
> I found him with a Rural Dean,
> Talking of district-visiting . . .
> The King is duller than the Queen.

Jacques Prévert (from Villon onwards, or from Hugh Primas
earlier still, the French have a firm line in the unrespectable)
changes the Lord's Prayer (p. 8) to

> Our Father who art in heaven
> Stay there.

The young Shelley (and much trouble it caused him) made
God declare (p. 9)

> From an eternity of idleness
> I, God awoke.

Poets especially victimize other poets. An exalted poet may in
various ways also seem ridiculous. Byron – necessarily much
comes from Byron, mocking decisively in the highest good
humour – jabbed at the soft spots in the poetry of Words-
worth (p. 282),

> We learn from Horace, 'Homer sometimes sleeps';
> We feel without him, Wordsworth sometimes wakes,–

and wasn't alone in that demonstration. Eliot – 'The lips seem
bursting with a deep Amen' – has appeared, to those qualified
to celebrate the fact, excessive or even ludicrous in one
direction or another (what must be in pickle now, somewhere,
for some poets of the Black Mountain?).

Our union of sexual divergence, our double-backed beast or double-backed delight – there is another subject which has always been fertile in unrespectable response, celebratory and condemnatory. Respectable hypocrisies as well are open always to mirth, directly or by implication; and the unrespectable handling in verse of all such matters of subject or concern can always be sharpened by the deliberate breaking of verbal taboos and by derisive unrespectability of manner; or by what amounts *per contra* to a derisive respectability of manner (I think, for example, of the way Oscar Wilde heightens the terror and disgrace of his great 'Ballad of Reading Gaol' – too familiar (and too long) to have in this collection – by setting the brutal in his once natural *fin de siècle* mannerism:

> It is sweet to dance to violins
>   When Love and Life are fair:
> To dance to flutes, to dance to lutes
>   Is delicate and rare:
> But it is not sweet with nimble feet
>   To dance upon the air!

– lines which occur not so far from the Governor in shiny black 'With the yellow face of Doom' or the warders creeping round the expectant prison in their felt shoes).

In the unrespectable poem the writer, I emphasize the fact, speaks out of his own mouth. At the top of the table of descent of such verse stand the *clerici vagantes* of the twelfth century, asserting a rhymed rhythmical individuality – yet still a limited individuality – in their Latin poems. When a final collection of the poems of Louis MacNeice came out after his death, how pleasurable it was to find that he had made the one good, if incomplete, translation of the 'Confession' of the Archpoet (p. 225) –

> Down the primrose path I trip, green and salad fashion,
> Virtue mine anathema, vice my only passion;

Less in love with heavenly joys than with pleasures sinful,
Dead in soul I save my skin, grant it many a skinful

– and how appropriate, since MacNeice exhibited in himself
and in his verse the kind of throwaway disrespect which
marked both the Archpoet of the Germans and that French
contemporary of his I have mentioned, the bitter and bawdy
Hugh Primas of Orléans (whom no poet has translated into
effective English?).

When the vernacular pushed Latin aside, individuality in-
creased and sharpened, in poets of the fourteenth and the
fifteenth centuries, in Dafydd ap Gwilym, in Villon (we are
lucky to have Villon translated so well by Swinburne, and my
friend the late Norman Cameron), even in Villon's gentle
associate, Charles Duke of Orléans in such a mild, charming
piece of unrespectability – if it is really by him – as 'My gostly
fadir, I me confess' (p. 94). I would not press for too much
individuality, too much raffish unrespectability in the author
of *Piers Plowman*; yet isn't there something more than the
moral view, something personal, in spite of himself, a certain
taste for the raffish, in spite of the way he condemns them, in
the lines (p. 214) about Gluttony and the companions of
Gluttony in the ale-house?

Since I have wished to underline the individuality of the
unrespectable, I haven't chosen for this book a great many
poems whose authors are unknown or uncertainly identified,
but what is apprehensible in Langland's 'laughing and louring
and "Let go the cuppe"' does recur in many such poems
which have their home strongly or faintly under the counter,
or are not, at any rate, to be recited on school speech-days.
From Scotland I have included that Breughel-like drawing,
the 'Blythsom Bridal' (p. 207), which may have been written
by the ballad maker Francis Sempill, and which is perhaps less
familiar than many Irish or English examples I could have
printed. Even the callousness and the violence you find in

some poems of the kind amount really to a caricature of evasion, a caricature of respectability. An example I could mention is the ballad of 'The Wednesbury Cocking', which Samuel Butler unexpectedly added to his *Alps and Sanctuaries*. The colliers and nailers of Wednesbury assemble at the cock-fight like the raffish in Gluttony's pub, and they eat, between the sport of the morning and the afternoon:

> The beef it was old and tough,
>   Off a bull that was baited to death,
> Burney Hyde got a lump in his throat,
>   That had like to have stopped his breath,
> The company all fell into confusion,
>   At seeing poor Barney Hyde choke;
> So they took him into the kitchen,
>   And held him over the smoke.
>
> They held him so close to the fire,
>   He frizzled just like a beef-steak,
> They then threw him down on the floor,
>   Which had like to have broken his neck.
> One gave him a kick on the stomach,
>   Another a kick on the brow,
> His wife said, Throw him into the stable,
>   And he'll be better just now.

– There's a poem Byron or amiable Chaucer or Rimbaud or E. E. Cummings, or Housman or Rochester, would have understood; or Yeats, who took much delight in the savage caricatural tales told by Sir Jonah Barrington in his *Personal Sketches*.

If I were to make a case against the satirist, reverting to that distinction, I would repeat that he is often the poet who deserts the occasionally unrespectable and starts regarding himself as the mouth of others who are like-minded; the poet who looks for self-justification in the un-selfcritical attitudes and *mores* of

an Establishment. This can be a fatal transition. I would in-
stance the South African poet Roy Campbell. In his 'Veld
Eclogue' (p. 253), which I find innocent and pleasurable when-
ever I read it again, he seems to me the momentarily unre-
spectable and disrespectful poet in high spirits, making fun of
the colonial or imperial ethos, the pioneering spirit, and the
like; impartially, between Boer and English –

> That they were true-bred children of the veld
> It could as easily be seen as smelt.

He comes to England, this poet, he is welcomed for his
energy and brio, but when found to be more rhetorical and
less intelligent than he had seemed, he senses the new, more
cautious attitude to himself, and changes; he begins to speak
in verse for a consensus of spiritual and political bullying –
with an inevitable degradation, and coarsening, and monoton-
izing, of his art.

I argue that the individual in his unrespectable poems speaks
one, if not two kinds of truth: he is himself, he voices himself
and his exasperation, his sense of the comic; he voices also his
sense of the disgraceful – or the comedy of the disgraceful;
he voices his sense of hypocrisy and false gods and unworthily
sacred cows. As the Muses say of themselves, via Hesiod, the
poet may know how to tell lies which seem true, when he
wishes; but he knows how to tell the things which are true.
The unrespectable poem which deserves respect, whatever its
occasion or its particular objective, derives, so I argue, from
an author's 'secrecy', or innerness, which is good; it tends to
that kind of truth, which is more than superficially truth to
the individual.

Of the poets I have known, I think often with regret, for the
goodness of his interior secrecy, of Norman Cameron, who
appears in this book in his own right and in his right as trans-
lator of Rimbaud and François Villon – by affinity. He was a

poet, in himself and in his verse, or in most of himself and what he said and wrote, who was organized round a core of incorruptibility; of which many stories are told, some of them expressing open-eyed surprise at the peculiarity of the behaviour of his contemporaries or acquaintances. He was an Edinburgh Scot, of Presbyterian upbringing, the son (I think) of a judge. 'Do you know what that girl told me she liked best in the world?' he said to me one day, of a considerable beauty we had recently encountered. 'The look in the eyes of schoolboys when she tosses them off in a train.'

He said this not as gossip, not as condemnation, but with surprise, at this revelation, from a girl who was as frank as himself, of the unexpected; and it is through knowing – or having known – that unrespectable poet, that acid for testing rightness, who made every one of his friends critical of his own attitudes and actions, that I believe I understand what it was that prompted the creation of many poems selected for this book, whether the writer was the Archpoet or Cavafy; Baudelaire or Tom Hood (whom Baudelaire admired); Rimbaud or Norman Cameron's own friend and master, Robert Graves. There are poems here present which I first heard of from Norman Cameron. E. E. Cummings's poem on Olaf the conscientious objector (p. 78) is one of them, another is John Crowe Ransom's 'Captain Carpenter' (p. 263); a third, 'The Inquest' by W. H. Davies (p. 139) – that poem of the dead female baby who seemed to wink with one eye open, one shut by a yellow lid.

In this book there are other poems written since Norman Cameron's death in 1953 – I have particularly in mind poems by Adrian Mitchell – which he would have enjoyed greatly. So I offer this collection to his memory; reflecting on one final aspect of the unrespectable in verse, its own quality of surprise, and its own frequent qualities of impudence and delightfulness of word, rhyme and situation. Villon's neck on the rope will learn the avoirdupois of his backside (p. 309); the Dean of St Paul's finds his beautiful wife – where? or how? – on Sir John Selby's bed, 'as flat as any flounder' (p. 93); Rochester will no longer 'drudge in fair Aurelia's womb' (p. 127) – and Southey, knocked down by St Peter, falls from heaven into his lake (p. 281), where (though not so worthless a poet as Byron maintained) he

> first sank to the bottom – like his works,
> But soon rose to the surface – like himself.

There are other kinds and springs of delightfulness, deeper, grander; but the unrespectable, that special form of the subversive, tests and confirms their nature. I trust few poets who have no gift for it.

GEOFFREY GRIGSON

P.S. Had permission to include them been given, there are just a few extra poems I would have included. I shall name them as a help to understanding my intentions in this anthology. They are – diversely – T. S. Eliot's 'Fragment of an Agon' (from *Sweeney Agonistes*); W. H. Auden's long early poem 'A Communist to Others', which was printed in *New Country;* and Buck Mulligan's 'Ballad of Joking Jesus', which was Oliver St John Gogarty's contribution to *Ulysses*. Also Rudyard Kipling's 'Common Form', one of his brief epitaphs, or epigrams, about the First World War. Buck Mulligan's ballad was my foundation stone – I mean, alas, it was the first poem I thought of for the anthology.

MATTERS OF GOD, HELL, AND HEAVEN

Mr Over

Mr Over is dead
He died fighting and true
And on his tombstone they wrote
Over to you.

And who pray is this You
To whom Mr Over is gone?
Oh if we only knew that
We should not do wrong.

But who is this beautiful You
We all of us long for so much
Is he not our friend and our brother
Our father and such?

Yes he is this and much more
This is but a portion
A sea-drop in a bucket
Taken from the ocean

So the voices spake
Softly above my head
And a voice in my heart cried: Follow
Where he has led

And a devil's voice cried: Happy
Happy the dead.

STEVIE SMITH

The Day After Sunday

Always on Monday, God's in the morning papers,
  His Name is a headline, His Works are rumoured abroad.
Having been praised by men who are movers and shapers,
  From prominent Sunday pulpits, newsworthy is God.

On page 27, just opposite Fashion Trends,
  One reads at a glance how He scolded the Baptists a little,
Was firm with the Catholics, practical with the Friends,
  To Unitarians pleasantly non-committal.

In print are His numerous aspects, too: God smiling,
  God vexed, God thunderous, God whose mansions are
     pearl,
Political God, God frugal, God reconciling
  Himself with science, God guiding the Camp Fire Girl.

Always on Monday morning the press reports
  God as revealed to His vicars in various guises –
Benevolent, stormy, patient, or out of sorts.
  God knows which God is the God God recognizes.

PHYLLIS MCGINLEY

There Is No God

(from *Dipsychus*)

'There is no God,' the wicked saith,
  'And truly it's a blessing,
For what He might have done with us
  It's better only guessing.'

4

'There is no God,' a youngster thinks,
  'Or really, if there may be,
He surely didn't mean a man
  Always to be a baby.'

'There is no God, or if there is,'
  The tradesman thinks, ''twere funny
If He should take it ill in me
  To make a little money.'

'Whether there be,' the rich man says,
  'It matters very little,
For I and mine, thank somebody,
  Are not in want of victual.'

Some others, also, to themselves,
  Who scarce so much as doubt it,
Think there is none, when they are well,
  And do not think about it.

But country folks who live beneath
  The shadow of the steeple;
The parson and the parson's wife,
  And mostly married people;

Youths green and happy in first love,
  So thankful for illusion;
And men caught out in what the world
  Calls guilt, in first confusion;

5

And almost every one when age,
   Disease, or sorrows strike him,
Inclines to think there is a God,
   Or something very like Him.

ARTHUR HUGH CLOUGH

The Latest Decalogue

Thou shalt have one God only; who
Would be at the expense of two?
No graven images may be
Worshipped, except the currency:
Swear not at all; for, for thy curse
Thine enemy is none the worse:
At church on Sunday to attend
Will serve to keep the world thy friend:
Honour thy parents; that is, all
From whom advancement may befall;
Thou shalt not kill; but need'st not strive
Officiously to keep alive:
Do not adultery commit;
Advantage rarely comes of it:
Thou shalt not steal; an empty feat,
When it's so lucrative to cheat:
Bear not false witness; let the lie
Have time on its own wings to fly:
Thou shalt not covet, but tradition
Approves all forms of competition.

ARTHUR HUGH CLOUGH

6

Poor People in Church

Between oak benches, in mean corners stowed away,
Warming the air with fetid breath, fixing their vision
On the gilt-dripping chancel's twenty mouths, which bray
The pious canticles with meaningless precision;

Sniffing the wax like fragrant bread, and revelling,
Like dogs that have been whipped, in their humiliation,
The Poor unto dear God, the master and the king,
Offer their laughable and stubborn supplication.

The women are well pleased to wear the benches smooth
After the six black days that God has just bestowed!
Tangled in curious swaddling-clothes, they rock and soothe
Their hardly-human babes, a weeping, fatal load.

Their grimy bosoms bared, these feeders upon soup,
With a prayer in their eyes, though they have never prayed,
Are watching the unseemly movements of a group
Of pert young girls, who in their battered hats parade.

Outside are cold and hunger, husbands on the booze.
Well, there's this hour; then come the evils without names.
Meanwhile, all round them, whining, snuffling, whispering
    news,
Sits a whole gathering of ancient, dewlapped dames.

The timid ones, the epileptic ones, from whom
Yesterday at the crossroads people turned aside,
The blind ones, nosing at old missals in the gloom,
Who creep into the courtyards with a dog for guide;

All, slavering their stupid beggars' creed, recite
Their endless plaint to Jesus, while he dreams on high
Beyond the murky window, in its yellowed light,
Far from thin evil ones, far from the fat and sly,

Far from the smells of meat, the smells of musty serge,
Prostrate and sombre farce in loathsome pantomime.
And now the worship blossoms with a keener urge,
The mysticalities become still more sublime,

When, coming from the nave through which no sunlight
    files,
Banal in silk, the Ladies of the town's best quarter
– O Christ! – the ones with liver-trouble and green smiles,
Offer bleached fingers to the kiss of holy-water.

ARTHUR RIMBAUD
(*translated by Norman Cameron*)

Pater Noster

Our Father who art in heaven
Stay there
And we'll stay here on earth
Which is sometimes so pretty
With its mysteries of New York
And its mysteries of Paris
At least as good as that of the Trinity
With its little canal at Ourcq
Its great wall of China
Its river of Morlaix
Its candy canes

8

With its Pacific Ocean
And its two basins in the Tuileries
With its good children and bad people
With all the wonders of the world
Which are here
Simply on the earth
Offered to everyone
Strewn about
Wondering at the wonder of themselves
And daring not avow it
As a naked pretty girl dares not show herself
With the world's outrageous misfortunes
Which are legion
With legionaries
With torturers
With the masters of this world
The masters with their priests their traitors and their troops
With the seasons
With the years
With the pretty girls and with the old bastards
With the straw of misery rotting in the steel
of cannons.

JACQUES PRÉVERT
(*translated by Lawrence Ferlinghetti*)

God and Man

(from *Queen Mab*)

'From an eternity of idleness
I, God, awoke; in seven days' toil made earth
From nothing; rested, and created man:

I placed him in a paradise, and there
Planted the tree of evil, so that he
Might eat and perish, and my soul procure
Wherewith to sate its malice, and to turn,
Even like a heartless conqueror of the earth,
All misery to my fame.   The race of men
Chosen to my honour, with impunity
May sate the lusts I planted in their heart.
Here I command thee hence to lead them on,
Until, with hardened feet, their conquering troops
Wade on the promised soil through woman's blood.
And make my name be dreaded through the land.
Yet ever-burning flame and ceaseless woe
Shall be the doom of their eternal souls,
With every soul on this ungrateful earth,
Virtuous or vicious, weak or strong – even all
Shall perish, to fulfil the blind revenge
(Which you, to men, call justice) of their God.'

       The murderer's brow
Quivered with horror.

          'God omnipotent,
Is there no mercy? must our punishment
Be endless? will long ages roll away,
And see no term?   Oh! wherefore hast thou made
In mockery and wrath this evil earth?
Mercy becomes the powerful – be but just
O God! repent and save.'

         'One way remains:
I will beget a son, and he shall bear
The sins of all the world; he shall arise
In an unnoticed corner of the earth,

And there shall die upon a cross, and purge
The universal crime; so that the few
On whom my grace descends, those who are marked
As vessels to the honour of their God,
May credit this strange sacrifice, and save
Their souls alive: millions shall live and die
Who ne'er shall call upon their Saviour's name,
But, unredeemed, go to the gaping grave.
Thousands shall deem it an old woman's tale,
Such as the nurses frighten babes withal:
These in a gulf of anguish and of flame,
Shall curse their reprobation endlessly,
Yet tenfold pangs shall force them to avow,
Even on their beds of torment, where they howl,
My honour, and the justice of their doom.
What then avail their virtuous deeds, their thoughts
Of purity, with radiant genius bright,
Or lit with human reason's earthly ray?
Many are called, but few will I elect.
Do thou my bidding, Moses!'

                    Even the murderer's cheek
Was blanched with horror, and his quivering lips
Scarce faintly uttered – 'O almighty one,
I tremble and obey!'

                                        P. B. SHELLEY

The Last Supper

They are at table
They eat not
Nor touch their plates
And their plates stand straight up
Behind their heads.

JACQUES PRÉVERT
(*translated by Lawrence Ferlinghetti*)

Lucifer

Lucifer did not wish to murder God,
But only to reduce His Self-esteem.
Weary of brightness where no shadow showed,
What took the rebel's fancy was a dream

Of God bewildered, angered out of measure
And driven, almost weeping, to implore,
'I built this Heaven for My angels' pleasure,
And yet you like it not. What would you more?'

At this, of course, with most Divine compassion,
Lucifer, all forgiving and adept,
Would soon have taught his Master how to fashion
A Heaven such as angels could accept.

NORMAN CAMERON

JOHN OLDHAM

from *Satires upon the Jesuits*

But nothing with the Crowd does more enhance
The value of these holy *Charlatans*,
Than when the Wonders of the Mass they view,
Where spiritual Jugglers their chief Mast'ry shew:
Hey Jingo, Sirs! What's this? 'tis Bread you see;
Presto be gone! 'tis now a Deity.
Two grains of Dough, with Cross, and stamp of Priest,
And five small words pronounc'd, make up their *Christ*.
To this they all fall down, this all adore,
And strait devour, what they ador'd before;
Down goes the tiny *Saviour* at a bit,
To be digested, and at length beshit:
From Altar to Close Stool, or Jakes preferr'd,
First Wafer, then a God, and then a turd.
'Tis this, that does the astonish'd Rout amuse,
And Reverence to shaven Crown infuse:
To see a silly, sinful, mortal Wight
His Maker make, create the Infinite.
None boggles at th'impossibility;
Alas, 'tis wondrous Heavenly Mystery! . . .

And here I might (if I but durst) reveal
What pranks are plaid in the Confessional:
How haunted Virgins have been dispossest,
And Devils were cast out, to let in Priest:
What Fathers act with Novices alone,
And what to Punks in shrieving seats is done;
Who thither flock to Ghostly Confessor,
To clear old debts, and tick with Heaven for more.
Oft have I seen these hallow'd Altars stain'd
With Rapes, those Pews with Buggeries profan'd: . . .

13

But I these dang'rous Truths forbear to tell,
For fear I should the Inquisition feel.
Should I tell all their countless Knaveries,
Their Cheats, and Shams, and Forgeries, and Lies,
Their Cringings, Crossings, Censings, Sprinklings, Chrisms,
Their Conjurings, and Spells, and Exorcisms;
Their Motly Habits, Maniples, and Stoles,
Albs, Ammits, Rochets, Chimers, Hoods, and Cowls;
Should I tell all their several Services,
Their Trentals, Masses, Dirges, Rosaries;
Their solemn Pomps, their Pageants, and Parades,
Their holy Masks, and spiritual Cavalcades,
With thousand Antick Tricks, and Gambols more;
'Twould swell the sum to such a mighty score,
That I at length should more volum'nous grow,
Than *Crabb*, or *Surius*, lying *Fox*, or *Stow*.
  Believe what e'er I have related here,
As true, as if 'twere spoke from Porph'ry Chair.
If I have feign'd in ought, or broach'd a Lie,
Let worst of Fates attend me, let me be
Pist on by Porter, Groom, and Oyster-whore,
Or find my Grave in Jakes, and Common-shore:
Or make next Bonfire for the *Powder-Plot*,
The sport of every sneering *Huguenot*.

JOHN OLDHAM

The Place of the Damn'd

All Folks, who pretend to *Religion* and *Grace*,
Allow there's a HELL, but dispute of the Place;
But, if HELL may by Logical Rules be defin'd
The Place of the Damn'd, – I'll tell you my Mind.

common-shore common sewer

14

Wherever the Damn'd do chiefly abound,
Most certainly there is HELL to be found;
Damn'd *Poets*, Damn'd *Criticks*, Damn'd *Blockheads*, Damn'd
  Knaves,
Damn'd *Senators* brib'd, Damn'd prostitute *Slaves*;
Damn'd *Lawyers* and *Judges*, Damn'd *Lords* and Damn'd
  Squires,
Damn'd *Spies* and *Informers*, Damn'd *Friends* and Damned
  Lyars;
Damn'd *Villains* corrupted in every *Station*;
Damn'd *Time-Serving Priests* all over the *Nation*.
And into the Bargain, I'll readily give ye,
Damn'd ignorant *Prelates*, and *Counsellors Privy*.
Then let us no longer by *Parsons* be flamm'd,
For We know by these *Marks*, the Place of the Damn'd:
And HELL to be sure is at *Paris* or *Rome*,
How happy for *Us*, that it is not at *Home!*

JONATHAN SWIFT

Punishment Enough

They say that women, in a bombing-raid,
Retire to sleep in brand-new underwear
Lest they be tumbled out of doors, displayed
In shabby garments to the public stare.

You've often seen a house, sliced like a cheese,
Displaying its poor secrets – peeling walls
And warping cupboards. Of such tragedies
It is the petty scale that most appals.

MATTERS OF GOD, HELL, AND HEAVEN

When you confess your sins before a parson,
You find it no great effort to disclose
Your crimes of murder, bigamy and arson,
But can you tell him that you pick your nose?

If after death you pay for your misdeeds,
Surely the direst and most just requital
Would be to listen while an angel reads
Before a crowd your endless, mean recital:

Golf scorecards faked, thefts from your mother's purse . . .
But why should Doomsday bother with such stuff?
This is the Hell that you already nurse
Within you. You've had punishment enough.

NORMAN CAMERON

On a Puritan

He served his God so faithfully and well
That now he sees him face to face, in hell.

HILAIRE BELLOC

Quite Apart from the Holy Ghost

I remember God as an eccentric millionaire,
Locked in his workshop, beard a cloud of foggy-coloured hair,
Making the stones all different, each flower and disease,
Putting the Laps in Lapland, making China for the Chinese,
Laying down the Lake of Lucerne as smooth as blue-grey lino,
Wearily inventing the appendix and the rhino,
Making the fine fur for the mink, fine women for the fur,
Man's brain a gun, his heart a bomb, his conscience – a blur.

ADRIAN MITCHELL

Christ I can see much better from here,
And Christ upon the Cross is clear.
Jesus is stretched like the skin of a kite
Over the Cross, he seems in flight
Sometimes. At times it seems more true
That he is meat nailed up alive and pain all through.
But it's hard to see Christ for priests. That happens when
A poet engenders generations of advertising men.

ADRIAN MITCHELL

Easter Day
Naples, 1849

Through the great sinful streets of Naples as I past,
With fiercer heat than flamed above my head
My heart was hot within me; till at last
My brain was lightened, when my tongue had said

    Christ is not risen!

  Christ is not risen, no,
  He lies and moulders low;
    Christ is not risen.

What though the stone were rolled away, and though
    The grave found empty there! –
    If not there, then elsewhere;
If not where Joseph laid Him first, why then
    Where other men
Translaid Him after; in some humbler clay
    Long ere to-day
Corruption that sad perfect work hath done,
Which here she scarcely, lightly had begun.

17

The foul engendered worm
Feeds on the flesh of the life-giving form
Of our most Holy and Anointed One.
    He is not risen, no,
    He lies and moulders low;
        Christ is not risen.
    Ashes to ashes, dust to dust;
As of the unjust, also of the just –
        Christ is not risen.

What if the women, ere the dawn was grey,
Saw one or more great angels, as they say,
Angels, or Him himself? Yet neither there, nor then,
Nor afterward, nor elsewhere, nor at all,
Hath He appeared to Peter or the Ten,
Nor, save in thunderous terror, to blind Saul;
Save in an after-Gospel and late Creed
    He is not risen indeed,
        Christ is not risen.

Or what if e'en, as runs the tale, the Ten
Saw, heard, and touched, again and yet again?
What if at Emmaüs' inn and by Capernaum's lake
    Came One the bread that brake,
Came One that spake as never mortal spake,
And with them ate and drank and stood and walked about?
    Ah! 'some' did well to 'doubt'!
Ah! the true Christ, while these things came to pass,
Nor heard, nor spake, nor walked, nor dreamt, alas!
    He was not risen, no,
    He lay and mouldered low,
        Christ was not risen.

As circulates in some great city crowd
A rumour changeful, vague, importunate, and loud,

From no determined centre, or of fact,
    Or authorship exact,
    Which no man can deny
    Nor verify;

    So spread the wondrous fame;
      He all the same
    Lay senseless, mouldering, low.
    He was not risen, no,
      Christ was not risen!
Ashes to ashes, dust to dust;
As of the unjust, also of the just –
    Yea, of that Just One too.
This is the one sad Gospel that is true,
    Christ is not risen.

*

Is He not risen, and shall we not rise?
    Oh, we unwise!
What did we dream, what wake we to discover?
Ye hills, fall on us, and ye mountains, cover!
    In darkness and great gloom
Come ere we thought it is *our* day of doom,
From the cursed world which is one tomb,
    Christ is not risen!

Eat, drink, and die, for we are men deceived,
Of all the creatures under heaven's wide cope
We are most hopeless who had once most hope,
We are most wretched that had most believed.
    Christ is not risen.

Eat, drink, and play, and think that this is bliss!
    There is no Heaven but this!

There is no Hell; –
Save Earth, which serves the purpose doubly well,
    Seeing it visits still
With equallest apportionments of ill
Both good and bad alike, and brings to one same dust
    The unjust and the just
    With Christ, who is not risen.

Eat, drink, and die, for we are souls bereaved,
Of all the creatures under this broad sky
We are most hopeless, that had hoped most high,
And most beliefless, that had most believed.
    Ashes to ashes, dust to dust;
    As of the unjust, also of the just –
        Yea, of that Just One too.
    It is the one sad Gospel that is true,
        Christ is not risen.

*

Weep not beside the Tomb,
    Ye women, unto whom
He was great solace while ye tended Him;
    Ye who with napkin o'er His head
And folds of linen round each wounded limb
    Laid out the Sacred Dead;
And thou that bar'st Him in thy Wondering Womb.
Yea, Daughters of Jerusalem, depart,
Bind up as best ye may your own sad bleeding heart;
Go to your homes, your living children tend,
    Your earthly spouses love;
    Set your affections *not* on things above,
Which moth and rust corrupt, which quickliest come to end:
Or pray, if pray ye must, and pray, if pray ye can,
For death; since dead is He whom ye deemed more than man,

Who is not risen, no,
But lies and moulders low,
    Who is not risen.

    Ye men of Galilee!
Why stand ye looking up to heaven, where Him ye ne'er may
        see,
Neither ascending hence, nor hither returning again?
    Ye ignorant and idle fishermen!
Hence to your huts and boats and inland native shore,
    And catch not men, but fish;
    Whate'er things ye might wish,
Him neither here nor there ye e'er shall meet with more.
    Ye poor deluded youths, go home,
    Mend the old nets ye left to roam,
    Tie the split oar, patch the torn sail;
    It was indeed 'an idle tale',
        He was not risen.

And oh, good men of ages yet to be,
Who shall believe *because* ye did not see,
    Oh, be ye warned! be wise!
    No more with pleading eyes,
    And sobs of strong desire,
  Unto the empty vacant void aspire,
Seeking another and impossible birth
That is not of your own and only Mother Earth.
But if there is no other life for you,
Sit down and be content, since this must even do:
        He is not risen.

    One look, and then depart,
    Ye humble and ye holy men of heart!
And ye! ye ministers and stewards of a word
Which ye would preach, because another heard, –

Ye worshippers of that ye do not know,
Take these things hence and go;
  He is not risen.

Here on our Easter Day
We rise, we come, and lo! we find Him not;
Gardener nor other on the sacred spot,
Where they have laid Him is there none to say!
No sound, nor in, nor out; no word
Of where to seek the dead or meet the living Lord;
There is no glistering of an angel's wings,
There is no voice of heavenly clear behest:
  Let us go hence, and think upon these things
  In silence, which is best.
    Is He not risen? No –
    But lies and moulders low –
      Christ is not risen.

ARTHUR HUGH CLOUGH

A Prayer

Searcher of souls, you who in heaven abide,
To whom the secrets of all hearts are open,
Though I do lie to all the world beside,
From me to thee no falsehood shall be spoken.
Cleanse me not, Lord, I say, from secret sin
But from these faults which he who runs can see.
'Tis these that torture me, O Lord, begin
With these and let the hidden vices be;
If you must cleanse these too, at any rate
Deal with the seen sins first, 'tis only reason,
They being so gross, to let the others wait

22

The leisure of some more convenient season;
   And cleanse not all even then, leave me a few.
   I would not be – not quite – so pure as you.

SAMUEL BUTLER

Mac Dhoul

I saw them all!
I could have laughed aloud
To see them at their capers;
That serious, solemn-footed, weighty crowd
Of angels – or, say, resurrected drapers!
Each with a thin flame swinging round his head!
With lilting wings and eyes of holy dread!
And curving ears strained for the great footfall!
And not a thought of sin – !
I don't know how I kept the laughter in.

For I was there!
Unknown, unguessed at! Snug
In a rose tree's branchy spurt!
With two weeks' whisker blackening lug to lug!
With tattered breeks and only half a shirt!
Swollen fit to burst with laughter at the sight
Of those dull angels, dropping left and right
Along the towering throne! Each in a scare
To hear His foot advance,
Huge from the cloud behind! All in a trance!

And suddenly,
As silent as a ghost,
I jumped out from the bush!

Went scooting through the glaring, nerveless host
All petrified, all gaping in a hush!
Came to the throne, and, nimble as a rat,
Hopped up it, squatted close, and there I sat,
Squirming with laughter till I had to cry,
To see Him standing there,
Frozen with all His angels in a stare!

He raised His hand!
His hand! 'Twas like a sky!
Gripped me in half a finger,
Flipped me round, and sent me spinning high
Through screaming planets! Faith, I didn't linger
To scratch myself! . . . And then adown I sped,
Scraping old moons and twisting, heels and head,
A chuckle in the void! Till . . . here I stand
As naked as a brick!
I'll sing the Peeler and the Goat in half a tick!

JAMES STEPHENS

I Reason, Earth Is Short

I reason, Earth is short,
And Anguish, absolute,
And many hurt,
But, what of that?

I reason, we could die,
The best Vitality
Cannot excel Decay,
But, what of that?

24

I reason, that in Heaven,
Somehow, it will be even,
Some new Equation, given,
But, what of that?

EMILY DICKINSON

ABOUT THOSE IN PLACE
OR AUTHORITY

Epitaph. For One Who Would Not Be Buried in Westminster Abbey

Heroes, and KINGS! your distance keep:
In peace let one poor Poet sleep,
Who never flatter'd Folks like you:
Let Horace blush, and Virgil too.

ALEXANDER POPE

The Courtier on Kings and the Poet's Reply
(from *The Satyres*)

... He adds, If of court life you knew the good,
You would leave lonenesse. I said, Not alone
My lonenesse is, but Spartanes fashion,
To teach by painting drunkards, doth not last
Now; Aretine's pictures have made few chast;
No more can Princes' courts, though there be few
Better pictures of vice, teach me vertue;
He, like to a high stretcht lute string squeakt, O Sir,
'Tis sweet to talke of Kings. At Westminster,
Said I, The man that keepes the Abbey tombes,
And for his price doth with who ever comes,
Of all our Harries, and our Edwards talke,
From King to King and all their kin can walke:
Your eares shall heare nought, but Kings: your eyes meet
Kings only; The way to it, is Kingstreet.

Aretine's pictures Aretino wrote poems to go with pornographic
engravings after Giulio Romano

He smack'd, and cry'd, He's base, Mechanique, coarse,
So are all your Englishmen in their discourse.
Are not your Frenchmen neate? Mine? as you see,
I have but one Frenchman, looke, hee followes mee.

JOHN DONNE

Ballade Tragique à Double Refrain

SCENE: A Room in Windsor Castle   TIME: The Present

Enter a Lady-in-Waiting and a Lord-in-Waiting

SHE: Slow pass the hours – ah, passing slow!
     My doom is worse than anything
    Conceived by Edgar Allan Poe:
     The Queen is duller than the King.

HE: Lady, your mind is wandering;
    You babble what you do not mean.
     Remember, to your heartening,
    The King is duller than the Queen.

SHE: No, most emphatically No!
     To one firm-rooted fact I cling
    In my now chronic vertigo:
     The Queen is duller than the King.

HE: Lady, you lie. Last evening
    I found him with a Rural Dean,
     Talking of district-visiting . . .
    The King is duller than the Queen.

Mechanique like a working man
neate elegant

SHE: At any rate he doesn't sew!
           You don't see *him* embellishing
         Yard after yard of calico . . .
             The Queen is duller than the King.
             Oh to have been an underling
         To (say) the Empress Josephine!

HE: Enough of your self-pitying!
         The King is duller than the Queen.

SHE (*firmly*): The Queen is duller than the King.

HE: Death then for you shall have no sting.

          [*Stabs her and, as she falls dead, produces phial from breast-pocket of coat.*]

          Nevertheless, sweet friend Strychnine,
          [*Drinks*]

          The King – is – duller than — the Queen.

          [*Dies in terrible agony.*]

MAX BEERBOHM

The Priapus King

(from *An Historical Poem*)

I. THE RESTORATION

Of a tall stature, and of sable hue,
Much like the son of Kish, that lofty Jew,
Twelve years complete he suffered in exile,
And kept his father's asses all the while;

At length, by wonderful impulse of fate,
The people call him home to help the state,
And, what is more, they send him money too,
And clothe him all, from head to foot, anew.
Nor did he such small favours then disdain,
Who in his thirtieth year began his reign:
In a slashed doublet then he came ashore,
And dubbed poor Palmer's wife his royal whore.
Bishops, and deans, peers, pimps, and knights, he made,
Things highly fitting for a monarch's trade!
With women, wine, and viands of delight,
His jolly vassals feast him day and night.
But the best times have ever some allay,
His younger brother died by treachery.
Bold James survives, no dangers make him flinch;
He marries Signor Falmouth's pregnant wench.
The pious mother queen, hearing her son
Was thus enamoured with a buttered bun,
And that the fleet was gone, in pomp and state,
To fetch, for Charles, the flowery Lisbon Kate,
She chants *Te Deum*, and so comes away,
To wish her hopeful issue timely joy.
Her most uxorious mate she ruled of old,
Why not with easy youngsters make as bold?

2. CHARLES AND HIS SISTER

The poor Priapus King, led by the nose,
Looks as a thing set up to scare the crows;
Yet, in the mimics of the spintrian sport,
Outdoes Tiberius, and his goatish Court.
In love's delights none did them e'er excel,
Not Tereus with his sister Philomel;

As they at Athens, we at Dover meet,
And gentlier far the Orleans Duchess treat.
What sad event attended on the same
We'll leave to the report of common fame.

ANDREW MARVELL

A Satyr on Charles II

I' th' isle of Britain, long since famous grown
For breeding the best cunts in Christendom,
There reigns, and oh! long may he reign and thrive,
The easiest King and best-bred man alive.
Him no ambition moves to get renown
Like the French fool, that wanders up and down
Starving his people, hazarding his crown.
Peace is his aim, his gentleness is such,
And love he loves, for he loves fucking much.
   Nor are his high desires above his strength:
His scepter and his prick are of a length;
And she may sway the one who plays with th' other,
And make him little wiser than his brother.
Poor prince! thy prick, like thy buffoons at Court,
Will govern thee because it makes thee sport.
'Tis sure the sauciest prick that e'er did swive,
The proudest, peremptoriest prick alive.
Though safety, law, religion, life lay on 't,
'Twould break through all to make its way to cunt.
Restless he rolls about from whore to whore,
A merry monarch, scandalous and poor.
   To Carwell, the most dear of all his dears,

Carwell Charles's mistress, Louise de Keroualle

The best relief of his declining years,
Oft he bewails his fortune, and her fate:
To love so well, and be beloved so late.
For though in her he settles well his tarse,
Yet his dull, graceless ballocks hang an arse.
This you'd believe, had I but time to tell ye
The pains it costs to poor, laborious Nelly,
Whilst she employs hands, fingers, mouth, and thighs,
Ere she can raise the member she enjoys.
   All monarchs I hate, and the thrones they sit on,
   From the hector of France to the cully of Britain.

JOHN WILMOT, EARL OF ROCHESTER

The Peerage of the Nation

(from *The True-Born Englishman*)

The Civil Wars, the common Purgative,
Which always use to make the Nation thrive,
Made way for all that strolling Congregation,
Which throng'd in Pious *Charles's* Restoration.
The *Royal Refugee* our Breed restores,
With *Foreign Courtiers*, and with *Foreign Whores*:
And carefully repeopled us again,
Throughout his Lazy, Long, Lascivious Reign;
The Labours of *Italian Castlemain*,
French Portsmouth, Taby Scot, and Cambrian.
Besides the Num'rous Bright and Virgin Throng,
Whole Female Glories shade them from my Song.
This Off-spring, if one Age they multiply,
May half the House with *English* Peers supply:

hang an arse hold back, i.e. won't do their job

34

There with true *English* Pride they may contemn
Schomberg and *Portland*, new made Noblemen.

French Cooks, *Scotch* Pedlars, and *Italian* Whores,
Were all made Lords, or Lords Progenitors.
Beggars and Bastards by his new Creation,
Much multiply'd the Peerage of the Nation;
Who will be all, e'er one short Age runs o'er,
As True-Born Lords as those we had before –

Then to recruit the Commons he prepares,
And heal the Latent Breaches of the Wars;
The Pious Purpose better to advance,
H'invites the banish'd Protestants of *France*:
Hither for God-sake and their own they fled,
Some for Religion came, and some for Bread:
Two hundred Thousand Pair of Wooden Shooes,
Who, God be thank'd had nothing left to lose;
To Heav'n's great Praise did for Religion fly,
To make us starve our Poor in Charity.
In ev'ry Port they plant their fruitful Train,
To get a Race of *True-Born* Englishmen:
Whose Children will, when Riper Years they see,
Be as Ill-natur'd and as Proud as we:
Call themselves *English*, Foreigners despise,
Be Surly like us all, and just as Wise.

Thus from a Mixture of all Kinds began,
That Het'rogeneous *Thing*, an *Englishman*:
In eager Rapes, and furious Lust begot,
Betwixt a Painted *Britain* and a *Scot*.

DANIEL DEFOE

Queens, Lesbians, Kings and Catamites

(from *The Authors of the Town*)

Queens, with their Ladies, work unseemly things,
And Boys grow Dukes, when Catamites to Kings.

RICHARD SAVAGE

The Georges

George the First was always reckoned
Vile, but viler George the Second;
And what mortal ever heard
Any good of George the Third?
When from earth the Fourth descended
(God be praised!) the Georges ended.

WALTER SAVAGE LANDOR

George the Third

(from *The Vision of Judgement*)

In the first year of freedom's second dawn
    Died George the Third; although no tyrant, one
Who shielded tyrants, till each sense withdrawn
    Left him nor mental nor external sun:
A better farmer ne'er brush'd dew from lawn,
    A worse king never left a realm undone!
He died – but left his subjects still behind,
One half as mad – and t'other no less blind.
He died! his death made no great stir on earth:
    His burial made some pomp; there was profusion
Of velvet, gilding, brass, and no great dearth
    Of aught but tears – save those shed by collusion.

36

For these things may be bought at their true worth;
   Of elegy there was the due infusion –
Bought also; and the torches, cloaks, and banners,
Heralds, and relics of old Gothic manners,

Form'd a sepulchral melodrame. Of all
   The fools who flock'd to swell or see the show,
Who cared about the corpse? The funeral
   Made the attraction, and the black the woe.
There throbb'd not there a thought which pierced the pall;
   And when the gorgeous coffin was laid low,
It seem'd the mockery of hell to fold
The rottenness of eighty years in gold.

So mix his body with the dust! It might
   Return to what it *must* far sooner, were
The natural compound left alone to fight
   Its way back into earth, and fire, and air;
But the unnatural balsams merely blight
   What nature made him at his birth, as bare
As the mere million's base unmummied clay –
Yet all his spices but prolong decay.

He's dead – and upper earth with him has done;
   He's buried; save the undertaker's bill,
Or lapidary scrawl, the world is gone
   For him, unless he left a German will:
But where's the proctor who will ask his son?
   In whom his qualities are reigning still,
Except that household virtue, most uncommon,
Of constancy to a bad, ugly woman.

GEORGE GORDON, LORD BYRON

The Duke of York's Statue

Enduring is the bust of bronze,
And thine, O flower of George's sons,
Stands high above all laws and duns.

As honest men as ever cart
Convey'd to Tyburn took thy part
And raised thee up to where thou art.

WALTER SAVAGE LANDOR

A Royal Duke

(from *Grotesques*)

A Royal Duke, with no campaigning medals
To dignify his Orders, he would speak
Nostalgically at times of Mozambique
Where once the ship he cruised in ran aground:
How he drank cocoa, from a sailor's mug,
Poured from the common jug,
While loyal toasts went round.

ROBERT GRAVES

Another Prince Is Born

Fire off the bells, ring out wild guns,
Switch on the sun for the son of sons.
For loyal rubbernecks to wait
Stick a notice on the gate.

Thrill to frill and furbelow,
God Save Sister Helen Rowe.
Lord Evans, Peel, Hall and Sir John
Guard the cot he dribbles on.
An angel in a Hunter jet
Circles round his bassinette.
Inform *The Times*, *Debrett*, *Who's Who*,
Better wake C. Day Lewis too.

Comes the parade of peers and peasants,
The Queen bears children, they bear presents –
Balls and toy guardsmen, well-trained parrots,
A regal rattle (eighteen carats),
And one wise man with myrrh-oiled hair
Brings a six-foot teddy bear
From the Birmingham Toy Fair.

ADRIAN MITCHELL

A Satirical Elegy

On the Death of a Late Famous General (The Duke of Marlborough)

His Grace! impossible! what dead!
Of old age too, and in his bed!
And could that Mighty Warrior fall?
And so inglorious, after all!
Well, since he's gone, no matter how,
The last loud trump must wake him now:
And trust me, as the noise grows stronger,
He'd wish to sleep a little longer.
And could he be indeed so old
As by the news-papers we're told?

Threescore, I think, is pretty high;
'Twas time in conscience he should die.
This world he cumber'd long enough;
He burnt his candle to the snuff;
And that's the reason, some folks think,
He left behind *so great a stink*.
Behold his funeral appears,
Nor widow's sighs, nor orphan's tears,
Wont at such times each heart to pierce,
Attend the progress of his herse.
But what of that, his friends may say,
He had those honours in his day.
True to his profit and his pride,
He made them weep before he dy'd.

Come hither, all ye empty things,
Ye bubbles rais'd by breath of Kings;
Who float upon the tide of state,
Come hither, and behold your fate.
Let pride be taught by this rebuke,
How very mean a thing's a Duke;
From all his ill-got honours flung,
Turn'd to that dirt from whence he sprung.

JONATHAN SWIFT

Providentially
right for once in his life-time
(his reasons were wrong),
the old sod was permitted
to save civilization.

W. H. AUDEN

40

GEORGE GORDON, LORD BYRON

Oh, Wellington!

(from *Don Juan*)

Oh, Wellington! (or 'Villainton' – for Fame
  Sounds the heroic syllables both ways;
France could not even conquer your great name
  But punn'd it down to this facetious phrase –
Beating or beaten she will laugh the same,)
  You have obtain'd great pensions and much praise:
Glory like yours should any dare gainsay,
Humanity would rise, and thunder 'Nay!'

I do n't think that you used Kinnaird quite well
  In Marinèt's affair – in fact 't was shabby,
And like some other things won't do to tell
  Upon your tomb in Westminster's old abbey.
Upon the rest 't is not worth while to dwell,
  Such tales being for the tea-hours of some tabby;
But though your years as *man* tend fast to *zero*,
In fact your grace is still but a *young hero*.

Though Britain owes (and pays you too) so much,
  Yet Europe doubtless owes you greatly more:
You have repair'd Legitimacy's crutch,
  A prop not quite so certain as before:
The Spanish, and the French, as well as Dutch,
  Have seen, and felt, how strongly you *restore;*
And Waterloo has made the world your debtor
(I wish your bards would sing it rather better).

You are 'the best of cut-throats:' – do not start;
  The phrase is Shakspeare's, and not misapplied: –
War's a brain-spattering, windpipe-slitting art,
  Unless her cause by right be sanctified.

41

If you have acted *once* a generous part,
   The world, not the world's masters, will decide,
And I shall be delighted to learn who,
Save you and yours, have gain'd by Waterloo?

I am no flatterer – you've supp'd full of flattery:
   They say you like it too – 't is no great wonder.
He whose whole life has been assault and battery,
   At last may get a little tired of thunder;
And swallowing eulogy much more than satire, he
   May like being praised for every lucky blunder,
Call'd 'Saviour of the Nations' – not yet saved,
And 'Europe's Liberator' – still enslaved.

I've done. Now go and dine from off the plate
   Presented by the Prince of the Brazils,
And send the sentinel before your gate
   A slice or two from your luxurious meals:
He fought, but has not fed so well of late.
   Some hunger, too, they say the people feels: –
There is no doubt that you deserve your ration,
But pray give back a little to the nation.

I do n't mean to reflect – a man so great as
   You, my lord duke! is far above reflection:
The high Roman fashion, too, of Cincinnatus,
   With modern history has but small connexion:
Though as an Irishman you love potatoes,
   You need not take them under your direction;
And half a million for your Sabine farm
Is rather dear! – I'm sure I mean no harm.

Great men have always scorn'd great recompenses:
   Epaminondas saved his Thebes, and died,

Not leaving even his funeral expenses:
  George Washington had thanks, and nought beside,
Except the all-cloudless glory (which few men's is)
  To free his country: Pitt too had his pride,
And as a high-soul'd minister of state is
Renown'd for ruining Great Britain gratis.

Never had mortal man such opportunity,
  Except Napoleon, or abused it more:
You might have freed fallen Europe from the unity
  Of tyrants, and been blest from shore to shore:
And *now* – what *is* your fame? Shall the Muse tune it ye?
  Now – that the rabble's first vain shouts are o'er?
Go! hear it in your famish'd country's cries!
Behold the world! and curse your victories!

As these new cantos touch on warlike feats,
  To *you* the unflattering Muse deigns to inscribe
Truths, that you will not read in the Gazettes,
  But which 't is time to teach the hireling tribe
Who fatten on their country's gore, and debts,
  Must be recited – and without a bribe.
You *did great* things: but not being *great* in mind,
Have left *undone* the *greatest* – and mankind.

Death laughs – Go ponder o'er the skeleton
  With which men image out the unknown thing
That hides the past world, like to a set sun
  Which still elsewhere may rouse a brighter spring –
Death laughs at all you weep for: – look upon
  This hourly dread of all! whose *threaten'd sting*
Turns life to terror, even though in its sheath:
Mark! how its lipless mouth grins without breath!

Mark! how it laughs and scorns at all you are!
  And yet *was* what you are; from *ear* to *ear*
It *laughs not* – there is now no fleshy bar
  So call'd; the Antic long hath ceased to *hear*,
But still he *smiles;* and whether near or far
  He strips from man that mantle (far more dear
Than even the tailor's), his incarnate skin,
White, black, or copper – the dead bones will grin.

And thus Death laughs, – it is sad merriment,
  But still it *is* so; and with such example
Why should not Life be equally content
  With his superior, in a smile to trample
Upon the nothings which are daily spent
  Like bubbles on an ocean much less ample
Than the eternal deluge, which devours
Suns as rays – worlds like atoms – years like hours?

'To be, or not to be? that is the question,
  Says Shakspeare, who just now is much in fashion.
I am neither Alexander nor Hephaestion,
  Nor ever had for *abstract* fame much passion;
But would much rather have a sound digestion,
  Than Buonaparte's cancer: – could I dash on
Through fifty victories to shame or fame,
Without a stomach – what were a good name?

'Oh dura ilia messorum!' – 'Oh
  Ye rigid guts of reapers!' I translate
For the great benefit of those who know
  What indigestion is – that inward fate
Which makes all Styx through one small liver flow.
  A peasant's sweat is worth his lord's estate:
Let *this* one toil for bread – *that* rack for rent,
He who sleeps best may be the most content.

44

'To be, or not to be?' – Ere I decide,
  I should be glad to know that which *is being;*
'T is true we speculate both far and wide,
  And deem, because we *see,* we are *all-seeing:*
For my part, I'll enlist on neither side,
  Until I see both sides for once agreeing.
For me, I sometimes think that life is death,
Rather than life a mere affair of breath.

'Que sçais je?' was the motto of Montaigne,
  As also of the first academicians;
That all is dubious which man may attain,
  Was one of their most favourite positions.
There 's no such thing as certainty, that 's plain
  As any of Mortality's conditions;
So little do we know what we 're about in
This world, I doubt if doubt itself be doubting.

It is a pleasant voyage perhaps to float,
  Like Pyrrho, on a sea of speculation;
But what if carrying sail capsize the boat?
  Your wise men do n't know much of navigation;
And swimming long in the abyss of thought
  Is apt to tire: a calm and shallow station
Well nigh the shore, where one stoops down and gathers
Some pretty shell, is best for moderate bathers.

'But heaven,' as Cassio says, 'is above all –
  No more of this, then, let us pray!' We have
Souls to save, since Eve's slip and Adam's fall,
  Which tumbled all mankind into the grave,
Besides fish, beasts, and birds. 'The sparrow's fall
  Is special providence,' though how it gave
Offence, we know not; probably it perch'd
Upon the tree which Eve so fondly search'd.

Oh! ye immortal Gods! what is theogony?
  Oh! thou, too, mortal man! what is philanthropy?
Oh! world, which was and is, what is cosmogony?
  Some people have accused me of misanthropy;
And yet I know no more than the mahogany
  That forms this desk, of what they mean; *lykanthropy*
I comprehend, for without transformation
Men become wolves on any slight occasion.

But I, the mildest, meekest of mankind,
  Like Moses, or Melancthon, who have ne'er
Done anything exceedingly unkind, –
  And (though I could not now and then forbear
Following the bent of body or of mind)
  Have always had a tendency to spare, –
Why do they call me misanthrope? Because
They hate me, not I them: – and here we'll pause.

'T is time we should proceed with our good poem, –
  For I maintain that it is really good,
Not only in the body but the proem,
  However little both are understood
Just now, – but by and by the Truth will show 'em
  Herself in her sublimest attitude:
And till she doth, I fain must be content
To share her beauty and her banishment.

GEORGE GORDON, LORD BYRON

Robin Hood and the Bishop of Hereford

Some they will talk of bold Robin Hood,
  And some of barons bold,
But I'll tell you how he servd the Bishop of Hereford,
  When he robbd him of his gold.

As it befel in merry Barnsdale,
  And under the green-wood tree,
The Bishop of Hereford was to come by,
  With all his company.

'Come, kill a venson,' said bold Robin Hood,
  'Come, kill me a good fat deer;
The Bishop of Hereford is to dine with me today,
  And he shall pay well for his cheer.

'We'll kill a fat venson,' said bold Robin Hood,
  'And dress it by the highway-side;
And we will watch the Bishop narrowly,
  Lest some other way he should ride.'

Robin Hood dressed himself in shepherd's attire,
  With six of his men also;
And, when the Bishop of Hereford came by,
  They about the fire did go.

'O what is the matter?' then said the Bishop,
  'Or for whom do you make this a-do?
Or why do you kill the king's venson,
  When your company is so few?'

'We are shepherds,' said bold Robin Hood,
  'And we keep sheep all the year,
And we are disposed to be merry this day,
  And to kill of the king's fat deer.'

'You are brave fellows!' said the Bishop,
  'And the king of your doings shall know;
Therefore make haste and come along with me,
  For before the king you shall go.'

'O pardon, O pardon,' said bold Robin Hood,
  'O pardon, I thee pray!
For it becomes not your lordship's coat
  To take so many lives away.'

'No pardon, no pardon,' says the Bishop,
  'No pardon I thee owe;
Therefore make haste, and come along with me,
  For before the king you shall go.'

Then Robin set his back against a tree,
  And his foot against a thorn,
And from underneath his shepherd's coat
  He pulld out a bugle-horn.

He put the little end to his mouth,
  And a loud blast did he blow,
Till threescore and ten of bold Robin's men
  Came running all on a row;

All making obeysance to bold Robin Hood;
  'T was a comely sight for to see:
'What is the matter, master,' said Little John,
  'That you blow so hastily?'

'O here is the Bishop of Hereford,
  And no pardon we shall have:'
'Cut off his head, master,' said Little John,
  'And throw him into his grave.'

'O pardon, O pardon,' said the Bishop,
  'O pardon, I thee pray!
For if I had known it had been you,
  I'd have gone some other way.'

ANONYMOUS

'No pardon, no pardon,' said Robin Hood,
  'No pardon I thee owe;
Therefore make haste and come along with me,
  For to merry Barnsdale you shall go.'

Then Robin he took the Bishop by the hand,
  And led him to merry Barnsdale;
He made him to stay and sup with him that night,
  And to drink wine, beer, and ale.

'Call in the reckoning,' said the Bishop,
  'For methinks it grows wondrous high:'
'Lend me your purse, Bishop,' said Little John,
  'And I'll tell you bye and bye.'

Then Little John took the bishop's cloak,
  And spread it upon the ground,
And out of the bishop's portmantua
  He told three hundred pound.

'Here's money enough, master,' said Little John,
  'And a comely sight 't is to see;
It makes me in charity with the Bishop,
  Tho he heartily loveth not me.'

Robin Hood took the Bishop by the hand,
  And he caused the music to play,
And he made the Bishop to dance in his boots,
  And glad he could so get away.

ANONYMOUS

A Quarrelsome Bishop

To hide her ordure, claws the cat;
You claw, but not to cover that.
Be decenter, and learn at least
One lesson from the cleanlier beast.

WALTER SAVAGE LANDOR

A Parson

(from *The Progress of a Divine*)

To preach o'er Beer, in *Burroughs*, to procure
Voters, to make the 'Squire's Election sure:
For this, where Clowns stare, gape, and grin, and baul,
Free to buffoon his Function to 'em all.
When the clod Justice some Horse-laugh wou'd raise,
Foremost the dullest of dull Jokes to praise;
To say, or unsay, at his Patron's Nod;
To do the *Will* of *All* – save that of *God*.
    His Int'rest the most servile Part he deems;
Yet much he sways, where much to serve he seems:
He sways his Patron, rules the Lady most,
And, as he rules the Lady, *rules the Roast.*
    Old Tradesmen must give Way to new – his Aim
Extorted *Poundage*, once the *Steward*'s Claim.
Tenants are rais'd; or, as his Pow'r encreases,
Unless they fine to Him, renew no Leases.
Thus Tradesmen, Servants, Tenants, none are free;
Their Loss and Murmur are his Gain and Glee.
    Lux'ry he loves; but, like a Priest of Sense,
Ev'n Lux'ry, loves not at his own Expence.

Though harlot Passions wanton with his Will,
Yet Av'rice is his wedded Passion still.
  See him with *Napkin*, o'er his *Band*, tuck'd in,
While the rich Grease hangs glist'ning on his Chin;
Or, as the *Dew* from *Aaron's* Beard declines,
Ev'n to his garment Hem, soft-trickling shines!
He feeds, and feeds, swills Soop, and sucks up Marrow;
Swills, sucks, and feeds, 'till leach'rous as a Sparrow.
Thy Pleasure, *Onan*, now no more delights;
The lone Amusement of his chaster Nights.
He boasts – (let Ladies put him to the Test!)
Strong Back, broad Shoulders, and a well-built Chest.
With stiff'ning Nerves, now steals he sly away;
Alert, warm, chuckling, ripe for am'rous Play;
Ripe, to caress the Lass; he once thought meet,
At Church to chide, when pennanc'd in a Sheet.
He pants, the titillating Joy to prove;
The fierce, short Sallies of luxurious Love.

RICHARD SAVAGE

Lord Coningsby's Epitaph

Here lies Lord Coningsby – Be civil!
The rest God knows – so does the Devil.

ALEXANDER POPE

I Met Murder on the Way

(from *The Mask of Anarchy*
Written on the Occasion of the Massacre at Manchester)

I

As I lay asleep in Italy
There came a voice from over the Sea,
And with great power it forth led me
To walk in the visions of Poesy.

II

I met Murder on the way –
He had a mask like Castlereagh –
Very smooth he looked, yet grim;
Seven blood-hounds followed him:

III

All were fat; and well they might
Be in admirable plight,
For one by one, and two by two,
He tossed them human hearts to chew
Which from his wide cloak he drew.

IV

Next came Fraud, and he had on,
Like Eldon, an ermined gown;
His big tears, for he wept well,
Turned to mill-stones as they fell.

V

And the little children, who
Round his feet played to and fro,
Thinking every tear a gem,
Had their brains knocked out by them.

VI

Clothed with the Bible, as with light,
And the shadows of the night,
Like Sidmouth, next, Hypocrisy
On a crocodile rode by.

VII

And many more Destructions played
In this ghastly masquerade,
All disguised, even to the eyes,
Like Bishops, lawyers, peers, or spies.

VIII

Last came Anarchy: he rode
On a white horse, splashed with blood;
He was pale even to the lips,
Like Death in the Apocalypse.

IX

And he wore a kingly crown;
And in his grasp a sceptre shone;
On his brow this mark I saw –
'I AM GOD, AND KING, AND LAW!'

X

With a pace stately and fast,
Over English land he passed,
Trampling to a mire of blood
The adoring multitude.

XI

And a mighty troop around,
With their trampling shook the ground,
Waving each a bloody sword,
For the service of their Lord.

XII

And with glorious triumph, they
Rode through England proud and gay,
Drunk as with intoxication
Of the wine of desolation.

XIII

O'er fields and towns, from sea to sea,
Passed the Pageant swift and free,
Tearing up, and trampling down;
Till they came to London town.

XIV

And each dweller, panic-stricken,
Felt his heart with terror sicken
Hearing the tempestuous cry
Of the triumph of Anarchy.

XV

For with pomp to meet him came,
Clothed in arms like blood and flame,
The hired murderers, who did sing
'Thou art God, and Law, and King.

XVI

'We have waited, weak and lone
For thy coming, Mighty One!
Our purses are empty, our swords are cold,
Give us glory, and blood, and gold.'

XVII

Lawyers and priests, a motley crowd,
To the earth their pale brows bowed:
Like a bad prayer not over loud,
Whispering – 'Thou art Law and God.' –

XVIII

Then all cried with one accord,
'Thou art King, and God, and Lord;
Anarchy, to thee we bow,
Be thy name made holy now!'

XIX

And Anarchy, the Skeleton,
Bowed and grinned to every one,
As well as if his education
Had cost ten millions to the nation.

XX

For he knew the Palaces
Of our Kings were rightly his;
His the sceptre, crown, and globe,
And the gold-inwoven robe.

XXI

So he sent his slaves before
To seize upon the Bank and Tower,
And was proceeding with intent
To meet his pensioned Parliament.

P. B. SHELLEY

Epitaph

Posterity will ne'er survey
A nobler grave than this:
Here lie the bones of Castlereagh:
Stop, traveller, and piss.

GEORGE GORDON, LORD BYRON

Hell – and London

(from *Peter Bell the Third*)

I

Hell is a city much like London –
  A populous and a smoky city;
There are all sorts of people undone,
And there is little or no fun done;
  Small justice shown, and still less pity.

II

There is a Castles, and a Canning,
  A Cobbett, and a Castlereagh;
All sorts of caitiff corpses planning
All sorts of cozening for trepanning
  Corpses less corrupt than they.

III

There is a ★ ★ ★, who has lost
  His wits, or sold them, none knows which;
He walks about a double ghost,
And though as thin as Fraud almost –
  Ever grows more grim and rich.

IV

There is a Chancery Court; a King;
  A manufacturing mob; a set
Of thieves who by themselves are sent
Similar thieves to represent;
  An army; and a public debt.

V

Which last is a scheme of paper money,
  And means – being interpreted –
'Bees, keep your wax – give us the honey,
And we will plant, while skies are sunny,
  Flowers, which in winter serve instead.'

VI

There is a great talk of revolution –
  And a great chance of despotism –
German soldiers – camps – confusion –
Tumults – lotteries – rage – delusion –
  Gin – suicide – and methodism;

VII

Taxes too, on wine and bread,
  And meat, and beer, and tea, and cheese,
From which those patriots pure are fed,
Who gorge before they reel to bed
  The tenfold essence of all these.

VIII

There are mincing women, mewing,
  (Like cats, who *amant miserè*,)
Of their own virtue, and pursuing
Their gentler sisters to that ruin,
  Without which – what were chastity?

IX

Lawyers – judges – old hobnobbers
  Are there – bailiffs – chancellors –
Bishops – great and little robbers –
Rhymesters – pamphleteers – stock-jobbers –
  Men of glory in the wars, –

X

Things whose trade is, over ladies
    To lean, and flirt, and stare, and simper,
Till all that is divine in woman
Grows cruel, courteous, smooth, inhuman,
    Crucified 'twixt a smile and whimper.

XI

Thrusting, toiling, wailing, moiling,
    Frowning, preaching – such a riot!
Each with never-ceasing labour,
Whilst he thinks he cheats his neighbour,
    Cheating his own heart of quiet.

XII

And all these meet at levees; –
    Dinners convivial and political; –
Suppers of epic poets; – teas,
Where small talk dies in agonies; –
    Breakfasts professional and critical;

XIII

Lunches and snacks so aldermanic
    That one would furnish forth ten dinners,
Where reigns a Cretan-tonguèd panic,
Lest news Russ, Dutch, or Alemannic
    Should make some losers, and some winners; –

XIV

At conversazioni – balls –
    Conventicles – and drawing-rooms –
Courts of law – committees – calls
Of a morning – clubs – book-stalls –
    Churches – masquerades – and tombs.

XV

And this is Hell – and in this smother
  All are damnable and damned;
Each one damning, damns the other;
They are damned by one another,
  By none other are they damned.

XVI

'Tis a lie to say, 'God damns!'
  Where was Heaven's Attorney General
When they first gave out such flams?
Let there be an end of shams,
  They are mines of poisonous mineral.

XVII

Statesmen damn themselves to be
  Cursed; and lawyers damn their souls
To the auction of a fee;
Churchmen damn themselves to see
  God's sweet love in burning coals.

XVIII

The rich are damned, beyond all cure,
  To taunt, and starve, and trample on
The weak and wretched; and the poor
Damn their broken hearts to endure
  Stripe on stripe, with groan on groan.

XIX

Sometimes the poor are damned indeed
  To take, – not means for being blessed, –
But Cobbett's snuff, revenge; that weed
From which the worms that it doth feed
  Squeeze less than they before possessed.

XX

And some few, like we know who,
  Damned – but God alone knows why –
To believe their minds are given
To make this ugly Hell a Heaven;
  In which faith they live and die.

XXI

Thus, as in a town, plague-stricken,
  Each man be he sound or no
Must indifferently sicken;
As when day begins to thicken,
  None knows a pigeon from a crow, –

XXII

So good and bad, sane and mad,
  The oppressor and the oppressed;
Those who weep to see what others
Smile to inflict upon their brothers;
  Lovers, haters, worst and best;

XXIII

All are damned – they breathe an air,
  Thick, infected, joy-dispelling:
Each pursues what seems most fair,
Mining like moles, through mind, and there
Scoop palace-caverns vast, where Care
  In thronèd state is ever dwelling.

P. B. SHELLEY

Where Is the World

(from *Don Juan*)

'Where is the world?' cries Young, at *eighty* – 'Where
　The world in which a man was born?' Alas!
Where is the world of eight years past? *'T was there* –
　I look for it – 't is gone, a globe of glass!
Crack'd, shiver'd, vanish'd, scarcely gazed on, ere
　A silent change dissolves the glittering mass.
Statesmen, chiefs, orators, queens, patriots, kings,
And dandies, all are gone on the wind's wings.

Where is Napoleon the Grand? God knows:
　Where little Castlereagh? The devil can tell:
Where Grattan, Curran, Sheridan, all those
　Who bound the bar or senate in their spell?
Where is the unhappy Queen, with all her woes?
　And where the Daughter, whom the Isles loved well?
Where are those martyr'd saints the Five per Cents?
And where – oh, where the devil are the Rents?

Where's Brumel? Dish'd. Where's Long Pole Wellesley?
　　Diddled.
　Where's Whitbread? Romilly? Where's George the Third?
Where is his will? (That's not so soon unriddled.)
　And where is 'Fum' the Fourth, our 'royal bird'?
Gone down, it seems, to Scotland to be fiddled
　Unto by Sawney's violin, we have heard:
'Caw me, caw thee' – for six months hath been hatching
This scene of royal itch and loyal scratching.

Where is Lord This? And where my Lady That?
　The Honourable Mistresses and Misses?
Some laid aside like an old Opera hat,

Married, unmarried, and remarried: (this is
An evolution oft perform'd of late).
Where are the Dublin shouts – and London hisses?
Where are the Grenvilles? Turn'd as usual. Where
My friends the Whigs? Exactly where they were.

Where are the Lady Carolines and Franceses?
Divorced or doing thereanent. Ye annals
So brilliant, where the list of routs and dances is, –
Thou Morning Post, sole record of the panels
Broken in carriages, and all the phantasies
Of fashion, – say what streams now fill those channels?
Some die, some fly, some languish on the Continent,
Because the times have hardly left them *one* tenant.

Some who once set their caps at cautious dukes,
Have taken up at length with younger brothers:
Some heiresses have bit at sharpers' hooks:
Some maids have been made wives, some merely mothers:
Others have lost their fresh and fairy looks:
In short, the list of alterations bothers.
There's little strange in this, but something strange is
The unusual quickness of these common changes.

Talk not of seventy years as age; in seven
I have seen more changes, down from monarchs to
The humblest individual under heaven,
That might suffice a moderate century through.
I knew that nought was lasting, but now even
Change grows too changeable, without being new:
Nought's permanent among the human race,
Except the Whigs *not* getting into place.

I have seen Napoleon, who seem'd quite a Jupiter,
    Shrink to a Saturn. I have seen a Duke
(No matter which) turn politician stupider,
    If that can well be, than his wooden look;
But it is time that I should hoist my 'blue Peter,'
    And sail for a new theme: – I have seen – and shook
To see it – the king hiss'd, and then carest;
But do n't pretend to settle which was best.

I have seen the Landholders without a rap –
    I have seen Joanna Southcote – I have seen
The House of Commons turn'd to a tax-trap –
    I have seen that sad affair of the late Queen –
I have seen crowns worn instead of a fool's cap –
    I have seen a Congress doing all that's mean –
I have seen some nations, like o'erloaded asses,
Kick off their burthens – meaning the high classes.

I have seen small poets, and great prosers, and
    Interminable – *not eternal* – speakers –
I have seen the funds at war with house and land –
    I have seen the country gentlemen turn squeakers –
I have seen the people ridden o'er like sand
    By slaves on horseback – I have seen malt liquors
Exchange for 'thin potations' by John Bull –
I have seen John half detect himself a fool –

But 'carpe diem,' Juan, 'carpe, carpe!'
    Tomorrow sees another race as gay
And transient, and devour'd by the same harpy.
    'Life's a poor player,' – then 'play out the play,
Ye villains!' and above all keep a sharp eye
    Much less on what you do than what you say:
Be hypocritical, be cautious, be
Not what you *seem*, but always what you *see*.

But how shall I relate in other cantos
  Of what befell our hero in the land,
Which 't is the common cry and lie to vaunt as
  A moral country? But I hold my hand –
For I disdain to write an Atalantis;
  But 't is as well at once to understand
You're *not* a moral people, and you know it
Without the aid of too sincere a poet.

GEORGE GORDON, LORD BYRON

A Short Song of Congratulation

Long-expected one and twenty
Ling'ring year at last is flown,
Pomp and Pleasure, Pride and Plenty
Great Sir John, are all your own.

Loosen'd from the Minor's tether,
Free to mortgage or to sell,
Wild as wind, and light as feather
Bid the slaves of thrift farewell.

Call the Bettys, Kates, and Jennys
Ev'ry name that laughs at Care,
Lavish of your Grandsire's guineas,
Show the Spirit of an heir.

All that prey on vice and folly
Joy to see their quarry fly,
Here the Gamester light and jolly
There the lender grave and sly.

Wealth, Sir John, was made to wander,
Let it wander as it will;
See the Jockey, see the Pander,
Bid them come, and take their fill.

When the bonny Blade carouses,
Pockets full, and Spirits high,
What are acres? What are houses?
Only dirt, or wet or dry.

If the Guardian or the Mother
Tell the woes of wilful waste,
Scorn their counsel and their pother,
You can hang or drown at last.

SAMUEL JOHNSON

Blue Blood

We thought at first, this man is a king for sure,
Or the branch of a mighty and ancient and famous lineage
– That silly, sulky, illiterate, black-avised boor
Who was hatched by foreign vulgarity under a hedge!

The good men of Clare were drinking his health in a flood,
And gazing, with me, in awe at the princely lad;
And asking each other from what bluest blueness of blood
His daddy was squeezed, and the pa of the da of his dad?

We waited there, gaping and wondering, anxiously,
Until he'd stop eating, and let the glad tidings out;
And the slack-jawed booby proved to the hilt that he
Was lout, son of lout, by old lout, and was da to a lout!

JAMES STEPHENS

An Ode to the Framers of the Frame Bill

I

Oh well done Lord E[ldo]n! and better done R[yde]r!
  Britannia must prosper with councils like yours;
Hawkesbury, Harrowby, help you to guide her,
  Whose remedy only must *kill* ere it cures:
Those villains; the Weavers, are all grown refractory,
  Asking some succour for Charity's sake –
So hang them in clusters round each Manufactory,
  That will at once put an end to *mistake*.

II

The rascals, perhaps, may betake them to robbing,
  The dogs to be sure have got nothing to eat –
So if we can hang them for breaking a bobbin,
  'T will save all the Government's money and meat:
Men are more easily made than machinery –
  Stockings fetch better prices than lives –
Gibbets on Sherwood will heighten the scenery,
  Shewing how Commerce, how Liberty thrives!

III

Justice is now in pursuit of the wretches,
  Grenadiers, Volunteers, Bow-street Police,
Twenty-two Regiments, a score of Jack Ketches,
  Three of the Quorum and two of the Peace;
Some Lords, to be sure, would have summoned the Judges
  To take their opinion, but that they ne'er shall,
For LIVERPOOL such a concession begrudges,
  So now they're condemned by *no Judges* at all.

IV

Some folks for certain have thought it was shocking,
  When Famine appeals and when Poverty groans,
That Life should be valued at less than a stocking,
  And breaking of frames lead to breaking of bones.
If it should prove so, I trust, by this token,
  (And who will refuse to partake in the hope?)
That the frames of the fools may be first to be *broken*,
  Who, when asked for a *remedy*, sent down a *rope*.

GEORGE GORDON, LORD BYRON

No Tenth Transmitter of a Foolish Face
(from *The Bastard*)

Blest be the *Bastard's* Birth! thro' wond'rous ways
He shines excentric like a Comet's Blaze!
No sickly Fruit of faint Compliance He!
He! stampt in Nature's Mint of Extacy!
He lives to build, not boast a generous Race:
No Tenth Transmitter of a foolish Face.
His daring Hope, no Sire's Example Bounds;
His First-born Lights no Prejudice Confounds.
He, kindling from within, requires no Flame;
He glories in a *Bastard's* glowing Name.
  Born to himself, by no Possession led,
In Freedom foster'd, and by Fortune fed;
Nor Guides, nor Rules, his Sov'reign Choice controul,
His Body Independent, as his Soul.
Loos'd to the World's wide Range, – enjoyn'd no Aim,
Prescrib'd no Duty, and assign'd no Name:
Nature's unbounded Son, he stands alone,
His Heart unbyass'd, and his Mind his own.

RICHARD SAVAGE

Mr Jones

'There's been an accident!' they said,
'Your servant's cut in half; he's dead!'
'Indeed!' said Mr Jones, 'and please
Send me the half that's got my keys.'

HARRY GRAHAM

MATTERS OF WAR

Evil

Whilst the red spittle of the grape-shot sings
All day across the endless sky, and whilst entire
Battalions, green or scarlet, rallied by their kings,
Disintegrate in crumpled masses under fire;

Whilst an abominable madness seeks to pound
A hundred thousand men into a smoking mess –
Pitiful dead in summer grass, on the rich ground
Out of which Nature wrought these men in holiness;

He is a God who sees it all, and laughs aloud
At damask altar-cloths, incense and chalices,
Who falls asleep lulled by adoring liturgies

And wakens when some mother, in her anguish bowed
And weeping till her old black bonnet shakes with grief
Offers him a big sou wrapped in her handkerchief.

ARTHUR RIMBAUD
(*translated by Norman Cameron*)

Look Down Fair Moon

Look down fair moon and bathe this scene,
Pour softly down night's nimbus floods on faces ghastly,
    swollen, purple,
On the dead on their backs with arms toss'd wide,
Pour down your unstinted nimbus sacred moon.

WALT WHITMAN

Hear Now the Tale of a Jetblack Sunrise

(from the first version of *Song of Myself*)

Hear now the tale of a jetblack sunrise,
Hear of the murder in cold blood of four hundred and twelve
  young men.

Retreating they had formed in a hollow square with their
  baggage for breastworks,
Nine hundred lives out of the surrounding enemy's nine times
  their number was the price they took in advance,
Their colonel was wounded and their ammunition gone,
They treated for an honorable capitulation, received writing
  and seal, gave up their arms, and marched back prisoners of
  war.

They were the glory of the race of rangers,
Matchless with a horse, a rifle, a song, a supper or a courtship,
Large, turbulent, brave, handsome, generous, proud and
  affectionate,
Bearded, sunburnt, dressed in the free costume of hunters,
Not a single one over thirty years of age.

The second Sunday morning they were brought out in squads
  and massacred . . . it was beautiful early summer,
The work commenced about five o'clock and was over by
  eight.

None obeyed the command to kneel,
Some made a mad and helpless rush . . . some stood stark and
  straight,
A few fell at once, shot in the temple or heart . . . the living
  and dead lay together,

The maimed and mangled dug in the dirt . . . the new-comers
  saw them there;
Some half-killed attempted to crawl away,
These were dispatched with bayonets or battered with the
  blunts of muskets;
A youth not seventeen years old seized his assassin till two
  more came to release him,
The three were all torn, and covered with the boy's blood.

At eleven o'clock began the burning of the bodies;
And that is the tale of the murder of the four hundred and
  twelve young men,
And that was a jetblack sunrise.

WALT WHITMAN

The Rear-Guard

(Hindenburg Line, April 1917)

Groping along the tunnel, step by step,
He winked his prying torch with patching glare
From side to side, and sniffed the unwholesome air.

Tins, boxes, bottles, shapes too vague to know,
A mirror smashed, the mattress from a bed;
And he, exploring fifty feet below
The rosy gloom of battle overhead.

Tripping, he grabbed the wall; saw some one lie
Humped at his feet, half-hidden by a rug,
And stooped to give the sleeper's arm a tug.
'I'm looking for headquarters.' No reply.

'God blast your neck!' (For days he'd had no sleep,)
'Get up and guide me through this stinking place.'
Savage, he kicked a soft, unanswering heap,
And flashed his beam across the livid face
Terribly glaring up, whose eyes yet wore
Agony dying hard ten days before;
And fists of fingers clutched a blackening wound.

Alone he staggered on until he found
Dawn's ghost that filtered down a shafted stair
To the dazed, muttering creatures underground
Who hear the boom of shells in muffled sound.
At last, with sweat of horror in his hair,
He climbed through darkness to the twilight air,
Unloading hell behind him step by step.

SIEGFRIED SASSOON

Trench Poets

I knew a man, he was my chum,
but he grew darker day by day,
and would not brush the flies away,
nor blanch however fierce the hum
of passing shells. I used to read,
to rouse him, random things from Donne –
like 'Get with child a mandrake-root.'
But you can tell he was far gone,
for he lay gaping, mackerel-eyed,
and stiff and senseless as a post
even when that old poet cried
'I long to talk with some old lover's ghost.'

I tried the *Elegies* one day,
but he, because he heard me say:
'What needst thou have more covering than a man?'
grinned nastily, so then I knew
the worms had got his brains at last.
There was one thing I still might do
to starve those worms; I racked my head
for wholesome things and quoted *Maud*.
His grin got worse and I could see
he sneered at passion's purity.
He stank so badly, though we were great chums
I had to leave him; then rats ate his thumbs.

EDGELL RICKWORD

Lamentations

I found him in the guard-room at the Base.
From the blind darkness I had heard his crying
And blundered in. With puzzled, patient face
A sergeant watched him; it was no good trying
To stop it; for he howled and beat his chest.
And, all because his brother had gone West,
Raved at the bleeding war; his rampant grief
Moaned, shouted, sobbed, and choked, while he was kneeling
Half-naked on the floor. In my belief
Such men have lost all patriotic feeling.

SIEGFRIED SASSOON

The Englishman's Home

I was playing golf the day
   That the Germans landed;
All our troops had run away,
   All our ships were stranded;
And the thought of England's shame
Altogether spoilt my game.

HARRY GRAHAM

Fight to a Finish

The boys came back. Bands played and flags were flying,
   And Yellow-Pressmen thronged the sunlit street
To cheer the soldiers who'd refrained from dying,
   And hear the music of returning feet.
'Of all the thrills and ardours War has brought,
This moment is the finest.' (So they thought.)

Snapping their bayonets on to charge the mob,
   Grim Fusiliers broke ranks with glint of steel.
At last the boys had found a cushy job.

     ★   ★   ★   ★   ★

I heard the Yellow-Pressmen grunt and squeal;
And with my trusty bombers turned and went
To clear those Junkers out of Parliament.

SIEGFRIED SASSOON

76

The Parable of the Old Men and the Young

So Abram rose, and clave the wood, and went,
And took the fire with him, and a knife.
And as they sojourned both of them together,
Isaac the first-born spake and said, My Father,
Behold the preparations, fire and iron,
But where the lamb for this burnt-offering?
Then Abram bound the youth with belts and straps,
And builded parapets and trenches there,
And stretchèd forth the knife to slay his son.
When lo! an angel called him out of heaven,
Saying, Lay not thy hand upon the lad,
Neither do anything to him. Behold,
A ram, caught in a thicket by its horns;
Offer the Ram of Pride instead of him.
But the old man would not so, but slew his son, –
And half the seed of Europe, one by one.

WILFRED OWEN

Familial

The mother does knitting
The son fights the war
She finds this quite natural the mother
And the father what does he do the father?
He does business
His wife does knitting
His son the war
He business
He finds this quite natural the father

77

And the son and the son
What does the son find the son?
He finds absolutely nothing the son
His mother does knitting his father business he war
When he finishes the war
He'll go into business with his father
The war continues the mother continues she knits
The father continues he does business
The son is killed he continues no more
The father and the mother go to the graveyard
They find this quite natural the father and mother
Life continues life with knitting war business
Business war knitting war
Business business business
Life with the graveyard.

JACQUES PRÉVERT
(*translated by Lawrence Ferlinghetti*)

i sing of Olaf glad and big
whose warmest heart recoiled at war:
a conscientious object-or

his wellbelovéd colonel (trig
westpointer most succinctly bred)
took erring Olaf soon in hand;
but – though an host of overjoyed
noncoms (first knocking on the head
him) do through icy waters roll
that helplessness which others stroke
with brushes recently employed
anent this muddy toiletbowl,
while kindred intellects evoke

allegiance per blunt instruments –
Olaf (being to all intents
a corpse and wanting any rag
upon what God unto him gave)
responds, without getting annoyed
'I will not kiss your f.ing flag'

straightway the silver bird looked grave
(departing hurriedly to shave)

but – though all kinds of officers
(a yearning nation's blueeyed pride)
their passive prey did kick and curse
until for wear their clarion
voices and boots were much the worse,
and egged the firstclassprivates on
his rectum wickedly to tease
by means of skilfully applied
bayonets roasted hot with heat –
Olaf (upon what were once knees)
does almost ceaselessly repeat
'there is some s. I will not eat'

our president, being of which
assertions duly notified
threw the yellowsonofabitch
into a dungeon, where he died

Christ (of His mercy infinite)
i pray to see; and Olaf, too

preponderatingly because
unless statistics lie he was
more brave than me: more blond than you.

E. E. CUMMINGS

The Enlisted Man

Yelled Colonel Corporal Punishment at Private Reasons:
  'Rebels like you have no right to enlist –
  Or to exist!'
Major Considerations leered approval,
  Clenching his fist,
  And gave his fierce moustache a fiercer twist.
So no appeal, even to General Conscience,
  Kept Private Reasons' name off the defaulter-list.

ROBERT GRAVES

Fifteen Million Plastic Bags

I was walking in a government warehouse
Where the daylight never goes.
I saw fifteen million plastic bags
Hanging in a thousand rows.

Five million bags were six feet long
Five million bags were five foot five
Five million were stamped with Mickey Mouse
And they came in a smaller size.

Were they for guns or uniforms
Or a dirty kind of party game?
Then I saw each bag had a number
And every bag bore a name.

And five million bags were six feet long
Five million were five foot five
Five million were stamped with Mickey Mouse
And they came in a smaller size.

So I've taken my bag from the hanger
And I've pulled it over my head
And I'll wait for the priest to zip it
So the radiation won't spread.

Now five million bags are six feet long
Five million are five foot five
Five million are stamped with Mickey Mouse
And they come in a smaller size.

ADRIAN MITCHELL

To Whom It May Concern

I was run over by the truth one day.
Ever since the accident I've walked this way
    So stick my legs in plaster
    Tell me lies about Vietnam.

Heard the alarm clock screaming with pain,
Couldn't find myself so I went back to sleep again
    So fill my ears with silver
    Stick my legs in plaster
    Tell me lies about Vietnam.

Every time I shut my eyes all I see is flames.
Made a marble phone book and I carved all the names
　　So coat my eyes with butter
　　Fill my ears with silver
　　Stick my legs in plaster
　　Tell me lies about Vietnam.

I smell something burning, hope it's just my brains.
They're only dropping peppermints and daisy-chains
　　So stuff my nose with garlic
　　Coat my eyes with butter
　　Fill my ears with silver
　　Stick my legs in plaster
　　Tell me lies about Vietnam.

Where were you at the time of the crime?
Down by the Cenotaph drinking slime
　　So chain my tongue with whisky
　　Stuff my nose with garlic
　　Coat my eyes with butter
　　Fill my ears with silver
　　Stick my legs in plaster
　　Tell me lies about Vietnam.

You put your bombers in, you put your conscience out,
You take the human being and you twist it all about
　　So scrub my skin with women
　　Chain my tongue with whisky
　　Stuff my nose with garlic
　　Coat my eyes with butter
　　Fill my ears with silver
　　Stick my legs in plaster
　　Tell me lies about Vietnam.

ADRIAN MITCHELL

MATTERS OF LOVE

Celia Celia

When I am sad and weary,
When I think all hope has gone,
When I walk along High Holborn
I think of you with nothing on.

Act Sederunt of the Session

A Scots Ballad

1

In Edinburgh town they've made a law,
  In Edinburgh at the Court o' Session
That standing pricks are fauteors a',
  And guilty of a high transgression. –

Act Sederunt o' the Session,
Decreet o' the Court o' Session,
That standing pricks are fauteors a',
And guilty of a high transgression.

2

And they've provided dungeons deep.
  Ilk lass has ane in her possession;
Until the wretches wail and weep,
  They there shall lie for their transgression. –

fauteors offenders

85

Act Sederunt o' the Session,
Decreet o' the Court o' Session,
The rogues in pouring tears shall weep,
By act Sederunt o' the Session.

ROBERT BURNS

I Have a Gentle Cock, Croweth Me Day

I have a gentle cock, croweth me day.
He doth me risen early my matins for to say.

I have a gentle cock, comen he is of gret,
His comb is of red coral, his tail is of jet.

I have a gentle cock, comen he is of kinde,
His comb is of red coral, his tail is of inde.

His legges ben of asor, so gentle and so smale,
His spores arn of silver white into the wortewale.

His eynen are of crystal loken all in aumber,
And every night he percheth him in mine lady's chaumber.

ANONYMOUS

gentle of good family
of gret from great (forebears)
of kinde from (good) kin
inde indigo
asor azure
spores spurs
wortewale skin at the root of the spur
eynen eyes
loken locked, set
aumber amber

86

Merrythought's Song

With hey trixie terlery-whiskin
    The world it runnes on wheeles
When the yong mans prick's in
    Up goes the maiden's heeles.

Sung in Beaumont and Fletcher's
Knight of the Burning Pestle

A Song of a Young Lady to her Ancient Lover

Ancient Person, for whom I
All the flatt'ring youth defy,
Long be it ere thou grow old,
Aching, shaking, crazy, cold;
But still continue as thou art,
Ancient Person of my heart.

On thy wither'd lips and dry,
Which like barren furrows lie,
Brooding kisses I will pour
Shall thy youthful heat restore
(Such kind showers in autumn fall,
And a second spring recall);
Nor from thee will ever part,
Ancient Person of my heart.

Thy nobler parts, which but to name
In our sex would be counted shame,
By age's frozen grasp possessed,
From their ice shall be released,

And, sooth'd by my reviving hand,
In former warmth and vigor stand.
All a lover's wish can reach
For thy joy my love shall teach,
And for thy pleasure shall improve
All that art can add to love.
Yet still I love thee without art,
Ancient Person of my heart.

JOHN WILMOT, EARL OF ROCHESTER

Niconoe and Priapus

Niconoe is inclined to deck
Thy ruddy shoulder and thick neck
    With her own fawn-skin, Lampsacene!
Beside, she brings a golden ewer
To cool thy hands in, very sure
    Among what herbage they have been.

Ah! thou hast wicked leering eyes,
And any maiden were unwise
    Who should invest thee face to face;
Therefore she does it from behind,
And blesses thee, so just and kind
    In giving her the prize for grace.

WALTER SAVAGE LANDOR

News for the Delphic Oracle

I

There all the golden codgers lay,
There the silver dew,
And the great water sighed for love,
And the wind sighed too.
Man-picker Niamh leant and sighed
By Oisin on the grass;
There sighed amid his choir of love
Tall Pythagoras.
Plotinus came and looked about,
The salt-flakes on his breast,
And having stretched and yawned awhile
Lay sighing like the rest.

II

Straddling each a dolphin's back
And steadied by a fin,
Those Innocents re-live their death,
Their wounds open again.
The ecstatic waters laugh because
Their cries are sweet and strange,
Through their ancestral patterns dance,
And the brute dolphins plunge
Until, in some cliff-sheltered bay
Where wades the choir of love
Proffering its sacred laurel crowns,
They pitch their burdens off.

III

Slim adolescence that a nymph has stripped,
Peleus on Thetis stares.
Her limbs are delicate as an eyelid,
Love has blinded him with tears;
But Thetis' belly listens.
Down the mountain walls
From where Pan's cavern is
Intolerable music falls.
Foul goat-head, brutal arm appear,
Belly, shoulder, bum,
Flash fishlike; nymphs and satyrs
Copulate in the foam.

W. B. YEATS

When a Man has Married a Wife, he finds out whether
Her knees & elbows are only glewed together.

WILLIAM BLAKE

The Question Answer'd

What is it men in women do require?
The lineaments of Gratified Desire.
What is it women do in men require?
The lineaments of Gratified Desire.

WILLIAM BLAKE

Riddle

Their tongues are knives, their forks are hands and feet.
They feed each other through their skins and eat
Religiously the spiced, symbolic meat.
The loving oven cooks them in its heat –
Two curried lovers on a rice-white sheet.

ADRIAN MITCHELL

The Thieves

Lovers in the act dispense
With such meum-teum sense
As might warningly reveal
What they must not pick or steal,
And their nostrum is to say:
I and you are both away.

After, when they disentwine
You from me and yours from mine,
Neither can be certain who
Was that I whose mine was you.
To the act again they go
More completely not to know.

Theft is theft and raid is raid
Though reciprocally made.
Lovers, the conclusion is
Doubled sighs and jealousies
In a single heart that grieves
For lost honour among thieves.

ROBERT GRAVES

In the Taverns

I wallow in the taverns   and in the brothels
of Beirut.   I did not want to remain
in Alexandria.   Tamides deserted me;
and he went off with the son   of the Eparch to acquire
a villa on the Nile,   a mansion in the city.
It wouldn't be right for me   to remain in Alexandria. –
I wallow in the taverns   and in the brothels
of Beirut.   I live abjectly
in shabby debauchery.   The only thing that saves me,
like a constant beauty,   like a fragrance that has
remained on my flesh,   is that I possessed Tamides
for two full years,   the most marvellous young man,
mine not merely for a house,   or a villa on the Nile.

FROM THE GREEK OF C. P. CAVAFY
(*translated by Rae Dalven*)

Inducas, inducas

Inducas, inducas,
In temptationibus.

The nun walked on her prayer,
    Inducas, inducas,
Ther cam a frer and met with her
    In temptationibus.

Inducas, inducas in temptationibus lead (us), lead (us) in temptations.
Parodied from the Lord's Prayer – *ne nos inducas in tentationem* lead us
not into temptation

This nun began to fall asleep,
    Inducas, inducas,
The frere kneeled down at her feet
    In temptationibus.

This frere began the nun to grope,
    Inducas, inducas,
It was a morsel for the Pope,
    In temptationibus.

The frere and the nun, whan they had done,
    Inducas, inducas,
Each to their cloister did they gone
    Sine temptationibus.

                        ANONYMOUS

Fragment of a Song on the Beautiful Wife of Dr John Overall, Dean of St Paul's

The Deane of Paule's did search for his wife
    And where d'ee thinke he found her?
Even upon Sir John Selbye's bed,
    As flatte as any flounder.

                        ANONYMOUS

sine without

Roundel: My Gostly Fadir I Me Confesse

My gostly fadir, I me confesse
First to God and then to yow
That at a wyndow wot ye how
I stale a cosse of gret swetnes
Which don was out avisynes.
But hit is doon, not undoon now,
 My gostly fadir, I me confesse
 First to God and then to yow.
But I restore it shalle dowtles
Ageyn if so be that I mow,
And that, God, I make a vow,
And ellis I axe foryefnes.
 My gostly fadir, I me confesse
 First to God and then to yow.

ASCRIBED TO CHARLES DUKE OF ORLÉANS

Figs

The proper way to eat a fig, in society,
Is to split it in four, holding it by the stump,
And open it, so that it is a glittering, rosy, moist, honied heavy-
 petalled four-petalled flower.

gostly fadir spiritual father, i.e. the priest
stale stole
cosse kiss
out avisynes without deliberation, on the spur of the moment
mow may

Then you throw away the skin
Which is just like a four-sepalled calyx,
After you have taken off the blossom with your lips.

But the vulgar way
Is just to put your mouth to the crack, and take out the flesh in
    one bite.

Every fruit has its secret.

The fig is a very secretive fruit.
As you see it standing growing, you feel at once it is symbolic:
And it seems male.
But when you come to know it better, you agree with the
    Romans, it is female.

The Italians vulgarly say, it stands for the female part; the fig-
    fruit:
The fissure, the yoni,
The wonderful moist conductivity towards the centre.

Involved,
Inturned,
The flowering all inward and womb-fibrilled;
And but one orifice.

The fig, the horse-shoe, the squash-blossom.
Symbols.

There was a flower that flowered inward, womb-ward;
Now there is a fruit like a ripe womb.

It was always a secret.
That's how it should be, the female should always be secret.

There never was any standing aloft and unfolded on a bough
Like other flowers, in a revelation of petals;
Silver-pink peach, venetian green glass of medlars and sorb-
   apples,
Shallow wine-cups on short, bulging stems
Openly pledging heaven:
Here's to the thorn in flower! Here is to Utterance!
The brave, adventurous rosaceae.

Folded upon itself, and secret unutterable,
And milky-sapped, sap that curdles milk and makes *ricotta*,
Sap that smells strange on your fingers, that even goats won't
   taste it;
Folded upon itself, enclosed like any Mohammedan woman,
Its nakedness all within-walls, its flowering forever unseen,
One small way of access only, and this close-curtained from
   the light;
Fig, fruit of the female mystery, covert and inward,
Mediterranean fruit, with your covert nakedness,
Where everything happens invisible, flowering and fertiliza-
   tion, and fruiting
In the inwardness of your you, that eye will never see
Till it's finished, and you're over-ripe, and you burst to give
   up your ghost.

Till the drop of ripeness exudes,
And the year is over.

And then the fig has kept her secret long enough.
So it explodes, and you see through the fissure the scarlet.
And the fig is finished, the year is over.

That's how the fig dies, showing her crimson through the
   purple slit

Like a wound, the exposure of her secret, on the open day.
Like a prostitute, the bursten fig, making a show of her secret.

That's how women die too.

The year is fallen over-ripe,
The year of our women.
The year of our women is fallen over-ripe.
The secret is laid bare.
And rottenness soon sets in.
The year of our women is fallen over-ripe.

When Eve once knew *in her mind* that she was naked
She quickly sewed fig-leaves, and sewed the same for the man.
She'd been naked all her days before,
But till then, till that apple of knowledge, she hadn't had the
    fact on her mind.

She got the fact on her mind, and quickly sewed fig-leaves.
And women have been sewing ever since.
But now they stitch to adorn the bursten fig, not to cover it.
They have their nakedness more than ever on their mind,
And they won't let us forget it.

Now, the secret
Becomes an affirmation through moist, scarlet lips
That laugh at the Lord's indignation.

What then, good Lord! cry the women.
We have kept our secret long enough.
We are a ripe fig.
Let us burst into affirmation.
They forget, ripe figs won't keep.
Ripe figs won't keep.

Honey-white figs of the north, black figs with scarlet inside, of
    the south.
Ripe figs won't keep, won't keep in any clime.
What then, when women the world over have all bursten into
    self-assertion?
And bursten figs won't keep?

San Gervasio

D. H. LAWRENCE

To Remain

It must have been one o'clock in the morning,
or half past one.

In a corner of the tavern;
behind the wooden partition.
Aside from the two of us the shop was completely deserted.
A kerosene lamp scarcely lighted it.
Dozing, at the doorway, the waiter dead for sleep.

No one would have seen us. But already
we had excited ourselves so much,
that we became unfit for precautions.

Our clothes were half opened – they were not many
for a divine month of July was scorching hot.

Enjoyment of the flesh between
our half-opened clothes;
quick baring of the flesh – the vision of what
occurred twenty-six years ago; and has now come
to remain among these verses.

FROM THE GREEK OF C. P. CAVAFY
(translated by Rae Dalven)

Hymn to Priapus

My love lies underground
With her face upturned to mine,
And her mouth unclosed in a last long kiss
That ended her life and mine.

I dance at the Christmas party
Under the mistletoe
Along with a ripe, slack country lass
Jostling to and fro.

The big, soft country lass,
Like a loose sheaf of wheat
Slipped through my arms on the threshing floor
At my feet.

The warm, soft country lass,
Sweet as an armful of wheat
At threshing-time broken, was broken
For me, and ah, it was sweet!

Now I am going home
Fulfilled and alone,
I see the great Orion standing
Looking down.

He's the star of my first beloved
Love-making.
The witness of all that bitter-sweet
Heart-aching.

Now he sees this as well,
This last commission.
Nor do I get any look
Of admonition.

He can add the reckoning up
I suppose, between now and then,
Having walked himself in the thorny, difficult
Ways of men.

He has done as I have done
No doubt:
Remembered and forgotten
Turn and about.

My love lies underground
With her face upturned to mine,
And her mouth unclosed in the last long kiss
That ended her life and mine.

She fares in the stark immortal
Fields of death;
I in these goodly, frozen
Fields beneath.

Something in me remembers
And will not forget.
The stream of my life in the darkness
Deathward set!

And something in me has forgotten,
Has ceased to care.
Desire comes up, and contentment
Is debonair.

I, who am worn and careful,
How much do I care?
How is it I grin then, and chuckle
Over despair?

Grief, grief, I suppose and sufficient
Grief makes us free
To be faithless and faithful together
As we have to be.

D. H. LAWRENCE

The Poet in a Fix

I came to a choice town with my handsome young servant:
all seemed clean and lively and a likely place for a good
supper which I enjoy like any other Welshman. I took a room
in the common inn . . . not a bad lodging . . . and called for
wine.

Then what should I see but a pretty slender girl in the house
. . . aha my pretty one! . . . such a bonny appearance, like the
rising sun even, drew my attention.

'I'll buy her a feast,' I thought, 'And some wine to give us
both courage'; it's a good game for young people inviting a
girl, however shy, to sit down beside you on the bench.

My luck was good, the whispered invitation put away her
shyness and we sat down to a feast, and if it had been a
wedding feast, they could scarcely have done us more honour.
And now I went more boldly with my whispering; (there is a
certain magic in two words, though contentment is not to be

had merely by adding a third:) whatever was said though, no one heard a word.

Love was not idle and it was arranged that I should come to the pretty creature when the company were all in bed. (She had dark hair, dark eyes and eyebrows.) When I considered, (what an idiot I was!) that all were asleep except the girl and I, I went with my usual expert cleverness to find the girl's bed. But then the trouble started!

I came upon a damned obstruction in the shape of three Englishmen in one stinking bed, pedlars with their three packs lying around . . . Hicken and Shockin and Shack or some such names. And then one of the scummy-mouthed louts started up in a monstrous rage and muttered to the other two, 'There's a Welshman creeping about in the dark on some trickery or other: he'll rob us if we let him, watch out for yourselves!' It's easy to be clumsy when you're in danger and I was not exactly nimble; as soon as I made a sound I brought down a fine lot of trouble on myself, it was not one of my better escapades. I bruised myself badly and hurt my leg and struck my shin against the edge of a stool, (O the ostler that left it in the way!) The stool creaked madly when my leg hit it. In my wretched haste I struck this and that and could find no clear course among the obstacles. Completely at sea, rushing here and there, I crashed my forehead against a table, down it fell and everything on it, down fell the trestles and all the other furniture, and then there was a basin that crashed down like a loud sounding gong. The noise that I made with the basin could be heard through the whole house; at the clang of the basin they set up a shout that there was some rogue here and all the dogs began to bark after me. The ostler roused the whole household . . . what a miserable tale . . . and they scowled around me in a circle searching and seeking for me while I, the poet, haggard now and wild, kept silent in the dark.

In hiding as I was, and a very frightened man, I prayed then with a bold prayer, and by the great charity and grace of Jesus I was delivered from my unlucky scrape and got myself back to my poor old bed. By the goodness of the Saints I escaped and may the Lord most High forgive me!

FROM THE WELSH OF DAFYDD AP GWILYM
(*translated by Nigel Heseltine*)

It Was a Maid of Brenten Arse

Sing dyllum, dyllum, dyllum, dyllum,
   I can tell you, and I will
   Of my lady's water-mill.

It was a maid of brenten arse,
She rode to mill upon a horse,
Yet was she maiden never the worse.

Laid was she upon a sack,
Strike soft, she said, hurt not my back,
And spare not, let the mill clack.

Iwis, the miller was full nice,
His millstones hanged by a vice
And would be walking at a trice.

brenten arse burnt arse, arse on fire
iwis certainly
full nice very lustful
vice screw
walking at a trice moving, turning straight away

This maid to mill did oft resort
And of her game made no report,
But to her it was full great comfort.

ANONYMOUS

The Reves Tale

At Trumpington, nat fer fro Cantebrigge,
Ther goth a brook and over that a brigge,
Up-on the whiche brook ther stant a melle;
And this is verray soth that I yow telle.
A Miller was ther dwelling many a day;
As eny pecok he was proud and gay.
Pypen he coude and fisshe, and nettes bete,
And turne coppes, and wel wrastle and shete;
And by his belt he baar a long panade,
And of a swerd ful trenchant was the blade.
A joly popper baar he in his pouche;
Ther was no man for peril dorste him touche.
A Sheffeld thwitel baar he in his hose;
Round was his face, and camuse was his nose.
As piled as an ape was his skulle.
He was a market-beter atte fulle.

pypen play the bagpipes
bete mend
coppes (wooden) cups
shete shoot
panade knife
popper dagger
thwitel long knife
camuse with a pug nose
piled bald
market-beter one who swaggers at market

Ther dorste no wight hand up-on him legge,
That he ne swoor he sholde anon abegge.
A theef he was for sothe of corn and mele,
And that a sly, and usaunt for to stele.
His name was hoten dëynous Simkin.
A wyf he hadde, y-comen of noble kin;
The person of the toun hir fader was.
With hir he yaf ful many a panne of bras,
For that Simkin sholde in his blood allye.
She was y-fostred in a nonnerye;
For Simkin wolde no wyf, as he sayde,
But she were wel y-norissed and a mayde,
To saven his estaat of yomanrye.
And she was proud, and pert as is a pye.
A ful fair sighte was it on hem two;
On haly-dayes biforn hir wolde he go
With his tipet bounden about his heed,
And she cam after in a gyte of reed;
And Simkin hadde hosen of the same.
Ther dorste no wight clepen hir but 'dame'.
Was noon so hardy that wente by the weye
That with hir dorste rage or ones pleye,
But-if he wolde be slayn of Simkin
With panade, or with knyf, or boydekin.
For jalous folk ben perilous evermo,

legge lay
abegge pay for it
usaunt accustomed
hoten dëynous jeering
person parson
gyte skirt
clepen call
rage maul about
ones only
boydekin dagger

105

Algate they wolde hir wyves wenden so.
And eek, for she was somdel smoterlich,
She was as digne as water in a dich;
And ful of hoker and of bisemare.
Hir thoughte that a lady sholde hir spare,
What for hir kinrede and hir nortelrye
That she had lerned in the nonnerye.

   A doghter hadde they bitwixe hem two
Of twenty yeer, with-outen any mo,
Savinge a child that was of half-yeer age;
In cradel it lay and was a propre page.
This wenche thikke and wel y-growen was,
With camuse nose and yën greye as glas;
With buttokes brode and brestes rounde and hye,
But right fair was hir heer, I wol nat lye.

   The person of the toun, for she was feir,
In purpos was to maken hir his heir
Bothe of his catel and his messuage,
And straunge he made it of hir mariage.
His purpos was for to bistowe hir hye
In-to som worthy blood of auncetrye;
For holy chirches good moot been despended
On holy chirches blood, that is descended.
Therfore he wolde his holy blood honoure,
Though that he holy chirche sholde devoure.

Algate, etc. always they would have it that wives go round that
     way
smoterlich having a bad name
digne repellent
hoker snootiness
bisemare disdain
nortelrye education
straunge he made it of he made difficulties about
good goods
moot been ought to be

106

Gret soken hath this miller, out of doute,
With whete and malt of al the land aboute;
And nameliche ther was a greet collegge,
Men clepen the Soler-halle at Cantebregge,
Ther was hir whete and eek hir malt y-grounde
And on a day it happed, in a stounde,
Sik lay the maunciple on a maladye;
Men wenden wisly that he sholde dye.
For which this miller stal bothe mele and corn
An hundred tyme more than biforn;
For ther-biforn he stal but curteisly,
But now he was a theef outrageously,
For which the wardeyn chidde and made fare.
But ther-of sette the miller nat a tare;
He craketh boost, and swoor it was nat so.

Than were ther yonge povre clerkes two,
That dwelten in this halle, of which I seye.
Testif they were, and lusty for to pleye,
And, only for hir mirthe and revelrye,
Up-on the wardeyn bisily they crye,
To yeve hem leve but a litel stounde
To goon to mille and seen hir corn y-grounde;
And hardily, they dorste leye hir nekke,
The miller shold nat stele hem half a pekke
Of corn by sleighte, ne by force hem reve;
And at the laste the wardeyn yaf hem leve.

soken right or toll (of milling)
nameliche especially
in a stounde once
wenden thought
made fare made a fuss
craketh boost talks big
testif headstrong
reve rob

John hight that oon, and Aleyn hight that other;
Of o toun were they born, that highte Strother,
Fer in the north, I can nat telle where.
  This Aleyn maketh redy al his gere,
And on an hors the sak he caste anon.
Forth goth Aleyn the clerk, and also John,
With good swerd and with bokeler by hir syde.
John knew the wey, hem nedede no gyde,
And at the mille the sak adoun he layth.
Aleyn spak first, 'al hayl, Symond, y-fayth;
How fares thy faire doghter and thy wyf?'
  'Aleyn! welcome,' quod Simkin, 'by my lyf,
And John also, how now, what do ye heer?'
  'Symond,' quod John, 'by god, nede has na peer;
Him boës serve him-selve that has na swayn,
Or elles he is a fool, as clerkes sayn.
Our manciple, I hope he wil be deed,
Swa werkes ay the wanges in his heed.
And forthy is I come, and eek Alayn,
To grinde our corn and carie it ham agayne;
I pray yow spede us hethen that ye may.'
  'It shal be doon,' quod Simkin, 'by my fay;
What wol ye doon whyl that it is in hande?'
  'By god, right by the hoper wil I stande,'
Quod John, 'and se how that the corn gas in;
Yet saugh I never, by may fader kin,

o one
him boës it behoves him
swayn young servant
hope fear
swa so
werkes ache
wanges molars
forthy therefore
hethen hence

108

How that the hoper wagges til and fra.'
   Aleyn answerde, 'John, and wiltow swa,
Than wil I be bynethe, by my croun,
And se how that the mele falles doun
In-to the trough; that sal be my disport.
For John, in faith, I may been of your sort;
I is as ille a miller as are ye.'
   This miller smyled of hir nycetee,
And thoghte, 'al this nis doon but for a wyle;
They wene that no man may hem bigyle;
But, by my thrift, yet shal I blere hir yë
For al the sleighte in hir philosophye.
The more queynte crekes that they make,
The more wol I stele whan I take.
In stede of flour, yet wol I yeve hem bren.
"The gretteste clerkes been noght the wysest men,"
As whylom to the wol thus spak the mare;
Of al hir art I counte noght a tare.'
   Out at the dore he gooth ful prively,
Whan that he saugh his tyme, softely;
He loketh up and doun til he hath founde
The clerkes hors, ther as it stood y-bounde
Behinde the mille, under a levesel;
And to the hors he gooth him faire and wel;
He strepeth of the brydel right anon.
And whan the hors was loos, he ginneth gon
Toward the fen, ther wilde mares renne,
Forth with wehee, thurgh thikke and thurgh thenne.

nycetee simple behaviour
nis doon but isn't done except
by my thrift if I can
queynte crekes smart tricks
levesel a leafy recess
wehee whinny

109

This miller gooth agayn, no word he seyde,
But dooth his note, and with the clerkes pleyde,
Til that hir corn was faire and wel y-grounde.
And whan the mele is sakked and y-bounde,
This John goth out and fynt his hors away,
And gan to crye 'harrow' and 'weylaway!
Our hors is lorn! Alayn, for goddes banes,
Step on thy feet, com out, man, al at anes!
Allas, our wardeyn has his palfrey lorn.'
This Aleyn al forgat, bothe mele and corn,
Al was out of his mynde his housbondrye.
'What? whilk way is he geen?' he gan to crye.

    The wyf cam leping inward with a ren,
She seyde, 'allas! your hors goth to the fen
With wilde mares, as faste as he may go.
Unthank come on his hand that bond him so,
And he that bettre sholde han knit the reyne.'

    'Allas,' quod John, 'Aleyn, for Cristes peyne,
Lay doun thy swerd, and I wil myn alswa;
I is ful wight, god waat, as is a raa;
By goddes herte he sal nat scape us bathe.
Why nadstow pit the capul in the lathe?
Il-hayl, by god, Aleyn, thou is a fonne!'

note work
harrow help
housbondrye household business
with a ren at a run
unthank a curse on
alswa as well
wight swift
raa roedeer
nadstow didn't you
capul horse
lathe barn
il-hayl curse (you)
fonne fool

This sely clerkes han ful faste y-ronne
To-ward the fen, bothe Aleyn and eek John.
　And whan the miller saugh that they were gon,
He half a busshel of hir flour hath take,
And bad his wyf go knede it in a cake.
He seyde, 'I trowe the clerkes were aferd;
Yet can a miller make a clerkes berd
For all his art; now lat hem goon hir waye.
Lo wher they goon, ye, lat the children pleye;
They gete him nat so lightly, by my croun!'
　Thise sely clerkes rennen up and doun
With 'keep, keep, stand, stand, jossa, warderere,
Ga whistle thou, and I shal kepe him here!'
But shortly, til that it was verray night,
They coude nat, though they do al hir might,
Hir capul cacche, he ran alwey so faste,
Til in a dich they caughte him atte laste.
　Wery and weet, as beste is in the reyn,
Comth sely John, and with him comth Aleyn.
'Allas,' quod John, 'the day that I was born!
Now are we drive til hething and til scorn.
Our corn is stole, men wil us foles calle,
Bathe the wardeyn and our felawes alle,
And namely the miller; weylaway!'
　Thus pleyneth John as he goth by the way
Toward the mille, and Bayard in his hond.
The miller sitting by the fyr he fond,

make a clerkes berd fool a clerk, a student
gete go
jossa down!
warderere ward rear, look out behind!
hething contempt
namely especially

For it was night, and forther mighte they noght;
But, for the love of god, they him bisoght
Of herberwe and of ese, as for hir peny.

  The miller seyde agayn, 'if ther be eny,
Swich as it is, yet shal ye have your part.
Myn hous is streit, but ye han lerned art;
Ye conne by argumentes make a place
A myle brood of twenty foot of space.
Lat see now if this place may suffyse,
Or make it roum with speche, as is youre gyse.'

  'Now, Symond,' seyde John, 'by seint Cutberd,
Ay is thou mery, and this is faire answerd.
I have herd seyd, man sal taa of twa thinges
Slyk as he fyndes, or taa slyk as he bringes.
But specially, I pray thee, hoste dere,
Get us som mete and drinke, and make us chere,
And we wil payen trewely atte fulle.
With empty hand men may na haukes tulle;
Lo here our silver, redy for to spende.'

  This miller in-to toun his doghter sende
For ale and breed, and rosted hem a goos,
And bond hir hors, it sholde nat gon loos;
And in his owne chambre hem made a bed
With shetes and with chalons faire y-spred,
Noght from his owne bed ten foot or twelve.
His doghter hadde a bed, al by hir-selve,

herberwe harbour, lodging
peny penny, money
roum roomy
gyse way, habit
taa take
slyk such
tulle entice
chalons blankets

112

Right in the same chambre, by and by;
It mighte be no bet, and cause why,
Ther was no roumer herberwe in the place.
They soupen and they speke, hem to solace,
And drinken ever strong ale atte beste.
Aboute midnight wente they to reste.

    Wel hath this miller vernisshed his heed;
Ful pale he was for-dronken, and nat reed.
He yexeth, and he speketh thurgh the nose
As he were on the quakke, or on the pose.
To bedde he gooth, and with him goth his wyf.
As any jay she light was and jolyf,
So was hir joly whistle wel y-wet.
The cradel at hir beddes feet is set,
To rokken, and to yeve the child to souke.
And whan that dronken al was in the crouke,
To bedde went the doghter right anon;
To bedde gooth Aleyn and also John;
Ther nas na more, hem nedede no dwale.
This miller hath so wisly bibbed ale,

by and by in due order, in turn
bet better
roumer herberwe roomier lodging
strong ale atte best strong ale at its best
vernisshed varnished
heed head
for-dronken very drunk, pissed
reed red
yexeth hiccoughs
were on the quakke, or on the pose had a sore throat or a cold in the head
yeve give
crouke crock, jug
dwale sleeping-draught
wisly assuredly

That as an hors he snorteth in his sleep,
Ne of his tayl behinde he took no keep.
His wyf bar him a burdon, a ful strong,
Men mighte hir routing here two furlong;
The wenche routeth eek *par companye.*

   Aleyn the clerk, that herd this melodye,
He poked John, and seyde, 'slepestow?
Herdestow ever slyk a sang er now?
Lo, whilk a compline is y-mel hem alle!
A wilde fyr up-on thair bodyes falle!
Wha herkned ever slyk a ferly thing?
Ye, they sal have the flour of il ending.
This lange night ther tydes me na reste;
But yet, na fors; al sal be for the beste.
For John,' seyde he, 'als ever moot I thryve,
If that I may, yon wenche wil I swyve.
Som esement has lawe y-shapen us;
For John, ther is a lawe that says thus,
That gif a man in a point be y-greved,
That in another he sal be releved.
Our corn is stoln, shortly, it is na nay,
And we han had an il fit al this day.

took no keep took no heed
bar him a burdon accompanied him in chorus
routing snoring
slyk such
whilk a compline what a compline, (evening service, last service
   of the day)
y-mel among
wilde fyr Greek fire
ferly wondrous, terrible
tydes me betides me
na fors it doesn't matter
swyve fuck
it is na nay there is no denying it

GEOFFREY CHAUCER

And sin I sal have neen amendement,
Agayn my los I wil have esement.
By goddes saule, it sal neen other be!'
   This John answerde, 'Alayn, avyse thee,
The miller is a perilous man,' he seyde,
'And gif that he out of his sleep abreyde
He mighte doon us bathe a vileinye.'
   Aleyn answerde, 'I count him nat a flye;'
And up he rist, and by the wenche he crepte.
This wenche lay upright, and faste slepte,
Til he so ny was, er she mighte espye,
That it had been to late for to crye,
And shortly for to seyn, they were at on;
Now pley, Aleyn! for I wol speke of John.
   This John lyth stille a furlong-wey or two,
And to him-self he maketh routhe and wo:
'Allas!' quod he, 'this is a wikked jape;
Now may I seyn that I is but an ape.
Yet has my felawe som-what for his harm;
He has the milleris doghter in his arm.
He auntred him, and has his nedes sped,
And I lye as a draf-sek in my bed;
And when this jape is tald another day,
I sal been halde a daf, a cokenay!
I wil aryse, and auntre it, by my fayth!
"Unhardy is unsely," thus men sayth.'

neen no
abreyde wake
auntred him took a risk
his nedes sped accomplished his business
draf-sek sack of chaff
daf fool
cokenay cissy
unhardy fainthearted
unsely unfortunate

115

And up he roos and softely he wente
Un-to the cradel, and in his hand it hente,
And baar it softe un-to his beddes feet.
   Sone after this the wyf hir routing leet,
And gan awake, and wente hir out to pisse,
And cam agayn, and gan hir cradel misse,
And groped heer and ther, but she fond noon.
'Allas!' quod she, 'I hadde almost misgoon;
I hadde almost gon to the clerkes bed.
Ey, *ben'cite!* thanne hadde I foule y-sped:'
And forth she gooth til she the cradel fond.
She gropeth alwey forther with hir hond,
And fond the bed, and thoghte noght but good,
By-cause that the cradel by its stood,
And niste wher she was, for it was derk;
But faire and wel she creep in to the clerk,
And lyth ful stille, and wolde han caught a sleep.
With-inne a whyl this John the clerk up leep,
And on this gode wyf he leyth on sore.
So, mery a fit ne hadde she nat ful yore;
He priketh harde and depe as he were mad.
This joly lyf han thise two clerkes lad
Til that the thridde cok bigan to singe.
   Aleyn wex wery in the daweninge,
For he had swonken al the longe night;
And seyde, 'far wel, Malin, swete wight!
The day is come, I may no lenger byde;
But evermo, wher so I go or ryde,

hente took
hir routing leet stopped her snoring
niste didn't know
ful yore for a very long while
swonken worked hard

116

I is thyn awen clerk, swa have I seel!'
  'Now dere lemman,' quod she, 'go, far weel!
But er thou go, o thing I wol thee telle,
Whan that thou wendest homward by the melle,
Right at the entree of the dore bihinde,
Thou shalt a cake of half a busshel finde
That was y-maked of thyn owne mele,
Which that I heelp my fader for to stele.
And, gode lemman, god thee save and kepe!'
And with that word almost she gan to wepe.
  Aleyn up-rist, and thoughte, 'er that it dawe,
I wol go crepen in by my felawe;
And fond the cradel with his hand anon,
'By god,' thoghte he, 'al wrang I have misgon;
Myn heed is toty of my swink to-night,
That maketh me that I go nat aright.
I woot wel by the cradel, I have misgo,
Heer lyth the miller and his wyf also.'
And forth he goth, a twenty devel way,
Un-to the bed ther-as the miller lay.
He wende have cropen by his felawe John;
And by the miller in he creep anon,
And caughte hym by the nekke, and softe he spak:
He seyde, 'thou, John, thou swynes-heed, awak
For Cristes saule, and heer a noble game.
For by that lord that called is seint Jame,

swa have I seel so happy I am
o one
al wrang I have misgon I've gone all the wrong way
toty dizzy from
swink work
a twenty devel way twenty devils' way
cropen crept

As I have thryes, in this shorte night,
Swyved the milleres doghter bolt-upright,
Whyl thow hast as a coward been agast.'
    'Ye, false harlot,' quod the miller, 'hast?
A! false traitour! false clerk!' quod he,
'Thou shalt be deed, by goddes dignitee!
Who dorste be so bold to disparage
My doghter, that is come of swich linage?'
And by the throte-bolle he caughte Alayn.
And he hente hym despitously agayn,
And on the nose he smoot him with his fest.
Doun ran the blody streem up-on his brest;
And in the floor, with nose and mouth to-broke,
They walwe as doon two pigges in a poke.
And up they goon, and doun agayn anon,
Til that the miller sporned at a stoon,
And doun he fil bakward up-on his wyf,
That wiste no-thing of this nyce stryf;
For she was falle aslepe a lyte wight
With John the clerk, that waked hadde al night.

swyved fucked
bolt-upright quite erect
agast afraid
harlot rogue
deed dead
throte-bolle Adam's apple
hente caught hold of
despitously angrily
to-broke bashed
poke sack
sporned tripped
stoon stone
a lyte wight a little while since

118

And with the fal, out of hir sleep she breyde –
'Help, holy croys of Bromeholm,' she seyde,
'*In manus tuas!* lord, to thee I calle!
Awak, Symond! the feend is on us falle,
Myn herte is broken, help, I nam but deed;
There lyth oon up my wombe and up myn heed;
Help, Simkin, for the false clerkes fighte.'
  This John sterte up as faste as ever he mighte,
And graspeth by the walles to and fro,
To finde a staf; and she sterte up also,
And knew the estres bet than dide this John,
And by the wal a staf she fond anon,
And saugh a litel shimering of a light,
For at an hole in shoon the mone bright;
And by that light she saugh hem bothe two,
But sikerly she niste who was who,
But as she saugh a whyt thing in hir yë.
And whan she gan the whyte thing espye,
She wende the clerk hadde wered a volupeer.
And with the staf she drough ay neer and neer,

breyde started
Bromeholm Broomholm Priory, Norfolk, a Cluniac house famous
    for a relic of the True Cross
in manus tuas into thy hands
I nam but deed I am almost dead
oon one
up on
wombe belly
estres insides
sikerly she niste she didn't really know
wende thought
volupeer nightcap
drough drew
neer nearer

And wende han hit this Aleyn at the fulle,
And smoot the miller on the pyled skulle,
That doun he gooth and cryde, 'harrow! I dye!'
Thise clerkes bete him weel and lete him lye;
And greythen hem, and toke hir hors anon,
And eek hir mele, and on hir wey they gon.
And at the mille yet they toke hir cake
Of half a busshel flour, ful wel y-bake.
    Thus is the proude miller wel y-bete,
And hath y-lost the grinding of the whete,
And payed for the soper every-deel
Of Aleyn and of John, that bette him weel.
His wyf is swyved, and his doghter als;
Lo, swich it is a miller to be fals!
And therfore this proverbe is seyd ful sooth,
'Him thar nat wene wel that yvel dooth;
A gylour shal him-self bigyled be.'
And God, that sitteth heighe in magestee,
Save al this companye grete and smale!
Thus have I quit the miller in my tale.

GEOFFREY CHAUCER

wende han thought to have
pyled bare
harrow help
greythen hem dressed themselves
every-deel every bit
als as well
ful sooth very truly
him thar nat wene wel that yvel dooth he must not expect much that
    evil doeth
gylour beguiler

Long John Brown and Little Mary Bell

Little Mary Bell had a Fairy in a nut,
Long John Brown had the Devil in his gut;
Long John Brown lov'd Little Mary Bell,
And the Fairy drew the Devil into the nut-shell.

Her Fairy skip'd out and her Fairy skip'd in;
He laugh'd at the Devil, saying 'Love is a sin.'
The Devil he raged and the Devil he was wroth,
And the Devil enter'd into the young man's broth.

He was soon in the gut of the loving young swain,
For John eat and drank to drive away love's pain;
But all he could do he grew thinner and thinner,
Tho' he eat and drank as much as ten men for his dinner.

Some said he had a wolf in his stomach day and night,
Some said he had the Devil and they guess'd right;
The Fairy skip'd about in his glory, joy and pride,
And he laugh'd at the Devil till poor John Brown died.

Then the Fairy skip'd out of the old nut-shell,
And woe and alack for Pretty Mary Bell!
For the Devil crept in when the Fairy skip'd out,
And there goes Miss Bell with her fusty old nut.

WILLIAM BLAKE

R.I.P.

A girl in our village makes love in the churchyard.
She doesn't care who, but it must be the churchyard.
They say she prefers the old part to the new.
Green granite chippings, maybe,
Rankle. Worn slabs welcome.
And after, in her bedroom,
She sees the mirror's view
Of her shoulder embossed
In Loving Memory.

Ann, why do you do it, you've eight 'O' Levels?
Why not, Ann? If bones remember, you'll give them joy.
It's as good a place as any,
Close by nave, rood screen and chapel at ease,
Peal of the bells,
Bob Singles and Grandsire Doubles,
And when you half close your eyes,
The horned gargoyles choose.

But it has to happen.
Oh, Ann, tonight you were levelled.
William Jones, late of this parish,
Was cold beneath you, and his great-great grandson
Warm above; and you rose,
Though your shoulder didn't know it,
In Glorious Expectation of the Life to Come.

ALAN GARNER

Winter Loving

Unhappy the man who is in love except in the summer, fruitless his prayers and great his desires. After the one night I had with the girl, all that is left me of that love-affair is my recollection of it, and the winter, I swear, is angry, black and bare after Christmas: and the snow, sure sign of the cold, and the frost and numerous icicles.

Coming drunk from the tavern, disgruntled and in a wretched humour, I went to look for her, terrified lest I find her making love to some other handsome man. Through the wood in the valley I went, feeling no love at all, till I arrived at the stone wall inside which the beauty lives.

There was a dismal sound of dripping from the eaves like an overflowing cheesepot; but when I arrived there I felt a kind of relief because of the danger close at hand beyond the wall. Thick under the edge of the cold roof were the frosty icicles, freezing cold, and cleverly the drops contrived to fall into my mouth as I stood at the mercy of the frost and the whistling rime of the ice. The frost bit me like a rake, and the cold went through me like the tender teeth of a harrow. As I stood in the porch the drops fell angrily on me from Jealousy's fine candles of ice, like freezing tears, and the snow drove every recollection out of me but that of black frost.

While my head endured the pangs of the drips from these cold spindles and the dismal sounds, I knocked on the window with my hand, hearing within the sounds of those in their first sleep, the man louder than the woman. Suspicious he nudged the pretty creature with his cold elbow, easily persuaded that someone was looking diligently for his money. Then the withered oaf rose out of his bed like a draught of foul air, enraged and terrified and calling 'Villain!' after me. And this was a dangerous journey for me, for he set a scound-relly pack on me consisting of the whole town; and he, promis-ing a candle to Mary at every sight of my footprints, bellowed after me with a hundred voices, 'After him there! he's bare-foot!'

So I fled with painful haste along the black back of the frost, till I came to the pleasant birch-wood which used to hide me in summer, thinking it to be, as I remembered it, a house of leaves under a fine roof, where the birds loved me and I saw the girl in May. But this was no trysting-place now, but a place of grief, even in the grove of the wood. No sign of love nor anything else did I see, nor any person nor any leaf, for the barren winter had winnowed the green warp of the leaves to the ground. And so I am begging May for a thaw before I freeze to death: I am a man imprisoned in winter; good luck to the summer and may it not be long coming!

FROM THE WELSH OF DAFYDD AP GWILYM
(*translated by Nigel Heseltine*)

Down, Wanton, Down!

Down, wanton, down! Have you no shame
That at the whisper of Love's name,
Or Beauty's, presto! up you raise
Your angry head and stand at gaze?

Poor bombard-captain, sworn to reach
The ravelin and effect a breach –
Indifferent what you storm or why,
So be that in the breach you die!

124

Love may be blind, but Love at least
Knows what is man and what mere beast;
Or Beauty wayward, but requires
More delicacy from her squires.

Tell me, my witless, whose one boast
Could be your staunchness at the post,
When were you made a man of parts
To think fine and profess the arts?

Will many-gifted Beauty come
Bowing to your bald rule of thumb,
Or Love swear loyalty to your crown?
Be gone, have done! Down, wanton, down!

ROBERT GRAVES

Women and Fools Are Always in Extreme

(from *Sober Advice from Horace, to the Young Gentlemen about Town*)

But why all this? I'll tell ye, 'tis my Theme:
'Women and Fools are always in Extreme.'
Rufa's at either end a Common-Shoar,
Sweet *Moll* and *Jack* are Civet-Cat and Boar:
Nothing in Nature is so lewd as *Peg*,
Yet, for the World, she would not shew her Leg!
While bashful *Jenny*, ev'n at Morning-Prayer,
Spreads her Fore-Buttocks to the Navel bare.
But diff'rent Taste in diff'rent Men prevails,
And one is fired by Heads, and one by Tails;
Some feel no Flames but at the *Court* or *Ball*,
And others hunt white Aprons in the *Mall*.

Common-Shoar common sewer

125

My Lord of *London*, chancing to remark
A *noted Dean* much busy'd in the Park,
'Proceed (he cry'd) proceed, my Reverend Brother,
'Tis *Fornicatio simplex*, and no other:
Better than lust for Boys, with *Pope* and *Turk*,
Or others Spouses, like my Lord of *York*.'

ALEXANDER POPE

On First Looking through Krafft-Ebing's Psychopathia Sexualis

Much have I travelled in those realms of old
Where many a whore in hall-doors could be seen
Of many a bonnie brothel or shebeen
Which bawds connived at by policemen hold.
I too have listened when the Quay was coaled,
But never did I taste the Pure Obscene –
Much less imagine that my past was clean –
Till this Krafft-Ebing out his story told.
Then felt I rather taken by surprise
As on the evening when I met Macran,
And retrospective thoughts and doubts did rise –
Was I quite normal when my life began
With love that leans towards rural sympathies
Potent behind a cart with Mary Ann?

OLIVER ST JOHN GOGARTY

Macran H. S. Macran, philosopher, of Trinity College, Dublin

annie died the other day

never was there such a lay –
whom, among her dollies, dad
first ('don't tell your mother') had;
making annie slightly mad
but very wonderful in bed
– saints and satyrs, go your way

youths and maidens: let us pray

E. E. CUMMINGS

Grown old in Love from Seven till Seven times Seven,
I oft have wish'd for Hell for Ease from Heaven.

WILLIAM BLAKE

Song

Love a woman? You're an ass!
   'Tis a most insipid passion
To choose out for your happiness
   The silliest part of God's creation.

Let the porter and the Groom,
   Things designed for dirty slaves,
Drudge in fair Aurelia's womb
   To get supplies for age and graves.

Farewell, woman! I intend
    Henceforth every night to sit
With my lewd, well-natured friend,
    Drinking to engender wit.

Then give me health, wealth, mirth, and wine,
    And, if busy love entrenches,
There's a sweet, soft page of mine
    Does the trick worth forty wenches.

JOHN WILMOT, EARL OF ROCHESTER

Against Constancy

Tell me no more of constancy,
    The frivolous pretense
Of cold age, narrow jealousy,
    Disease, and want of sense.

Let duller fools, on whom kind chance
    Some easy heart has thrown,
Despairing higher to advance,
    Be kind to one alone.

Old men and weak, whose idle flame
    Their own defects discovers,
Since changing can but spread their shame,
    Ought to be constant lovers.

But we, whose hearts do justly swell
    With no vainglorious pride,
Who know how we in love excel,
    Long to be often tried.

Then bring my bath, and strew my bed,
   As each kind night returns;
I'll change a mistress till I'm dead –
   And fate change me to worms.

A Fragment of Petronius Paraphras'd

Faeda est in coitu, et brevis voluptas, etc.

I hate Fruition, now 'tis past,
'Tis all but nastiness at best;
The homeliest thing, that Man can do
Besides, 'tis short, and fleeting too:
A squirt of slippery Delight,
That with a moment takes its flight,
A fulsom Bliss, that soon does cloy,
And make us loath what we enjoy.
Then let us not too eager run,
By Passion blindly hurried on,
Like Beasts who nothing better know,
Than what meer Lust incites them to:
For when in Floods of Love we're drench'd,
The Flames are by enjoyment quench'd:
But thus, let's thus together lie,
And kiss out long Eternity:
Here we dread no conscious spies,
No blushes stain our guiltless Joys:
Here no faintness dulls Desires,
And Pleasure never flags, nor tires:

This has pleas'd, and pleases now,
And for Ages will do so:
  Enjoyment here is never done,
  But fresh, and always but begun.

JOHN OLDHAM

His Treacherous Member

(from *The Imperfect Enjoyment*)

Thou treacherous, base deserter of my flame,
False to my passion, fatal to my fame,
Through what mistaken magic dost thou prove
So true to lewdness, so untrue to love?
What oyster-cinder-beggar-common whore
Didst thou e'er fail in all thy life before?
When vice, disease, and scandal lead the way,
With what officious haste dost thou obey!
Like a rude, roaring hector in the streets
Who scuffles, cuffs, and justles all he meets,
But if his King or country claim his aid,
The rakehell villain shrinks and hides his head;
Ev'n so thy brutal valor is displayed,
Breaks every stew, does each small whore invade,
But when great Love the onset does command,
Base recreant to thy prince, thou dar'st not stand.
Worst part of me, and henceforth hated most,
Through all the town a common fucking post,
On whom each whore relieves her tingling cunt
As hogs on gates do rub themselves and grunt,
Mayst thou to ravenous chancres be a prey,
Or in consuming weepings waste away;

May strangury and stone thy days attend;
May'st thou ne'er piss, who didst refuse to spend
When all my joys did on false thee depend.
　　And may ten thousand abler pricks agree
　　To do the wronged Corinna right for thee.

JOHN WILMOT, EARL OF ROCHESTER

Anne, Turning Nun

Exhausted now her sighs, and dry her tears,
For twenty youths these more than twenty years,
Anne, turning nun, swears God alone shall have her ...
God ought to bow profoundly for the favour.

WALTER SAVAGE LANDOR

On Mrs Willis

　　Against the charms our ballocks have
　　　　How weak all human skill is,
　　Since they can make a man a slave
　　　　To such a bitch as Willis!

　　Whom that I may describe throughout,
　　　　Assist me, bawdy powers;
　　I'll write upon a double clout,
　　　　And dip my pen in flowers.

spend come
double clout folded rag used as sanitary towel
flowers menses

Her look's demurely impudent,
　　Ungainly beautiful;
Her modesty is insolent,
　　Her wit both pert and dull.

A prostitute to all the town,
　　And yet with no man friends,
She rails and scolds when she lies down,
　　And curses when she spends.

Bawdy in thoughts, precise in words,
　　Ill-natured though a whore,
Her belly is a bag of turds,
　　And her cunt a common shore.

JOHN WILMOT, EARL OF ROCHESTER

The Disabled Debauchee

As some brave admiral, in former war
　　Deprived of force, but pressed with courage still,
Two rival fleets appearing from afar,
　　Crawls to the top of an adjacent hill;

From whence, with thoughts full of concern, he views
　　The wise and daring conduct of the fight,
Whilst each bold action to his mind renews
　　His present glory and his past delight;

spends has her orgasm
common shore common sewer

From his fierce eyes flashes of fire he throws,
  As from black clouds when lightning breaks away;
Transported, thinks himself amidst the foes,
  And absent, yet enjoys the bloody day;

So, when my days of impotence approach,
  And I'm by pox and wine's unlucky chance
Forced from the pleasing billows of debauch
  On the dull shore of lazy temperance,

My pains at least some respite shall afford
  While I behold the battles you maintain
When fleets of glasses sail about the board,
  From whose broadsides volleys of wit shall rain.

Nor let the sight of honorable scars,
  Which my too forward valor did procure,
Frighten new-listed soldiers from the wars:
  Past joys have more than paid what I endure.

Should any youth (worth being drunk) prove nice,
  And from his fair inviter meanly shrink,
'Twill please the ghost of my departed vice
  If, at my counsel, he repent and drink.

Or should some cold-complexioned sot forbid,
  With his dull morals, our bold night-alarms,
I'll fire his blood by telling what I did
  When I was strong, and able to bear arms.

I'll tell of whores attacked, their lords at home;
  Bawds' quarters beaten up, and fortress won;
Windows demolished, watches overcome;
  And handsome ills by my contrivance done.

Nor shall our love-fits, Chloris, be forgot,
    When each the well-looked linkboy strove t' enjoy,
And the best kiss was the deciding lot
    Whether the boy fucked you, or I the boy.

With tales like these I will such thoughts inspire
    As to important mischief shall incline:
I'll make him long some ancient church to fire,
    And fear no lewdness he's called to by wine.

Thus, statesmanlike, I'll saucily impose,
    And safe from action, valiantly advise;
Sheltered in impotence, urge you to blows,
    And, being good for nothing else, be wise.

JOHN WILMOT, EARL OF ROCHESTER

A Last Confession

What lively lad most pleasured me
Of all that with me lay?
I answer that I gave my soul
And loved in misery,
But had great pleasure with a lad
That I loved bodily.

Flinging from his arms I laughed
To think his passion such
He fancied that I gave a soul
Did but our bodies touch,
And laughed upon his breast to think
Beast gave beast as much.

I gave what other women gave
That stepped out of their clothes,
But when this soul, its body off,
Naked to naked goes,
He it has found shall find therein
What none other knows,

And give his own and take his own
And rule in his own right;
And though it loved in misery
Close and cling so tight,
There's not a bird of day that dare
Extinguish that delight.

W. B. YEATS

MATTERS OF JUSTICE, TRUTH, AND THE POOR

The Inquest

I took my oath I would enquire,
  Without affection, hate, or wrath,
Into the death of Ada Wright –
  So help me God! I took that oath.

When I went out to see the corpse,
  The four months babe that died so young,
I judged it was seven pounds in weight,
  And little more than one foot long.

One eye, that had a yellow lid,
  Was shut – so was the mouth, that smiled;
The left eye open, shining bright –
  It seemed a knowing little child.

For as I looked at that one eye,
  It seemed to laugh, and say with glee:
'What caused my death you'll never know –
  Perhaps my mother murdered me.'

When I went into court again,
  To hear the mother's evidence –
It was a love-child, she explained,
  And smiled, for our intelligence.

'Now, Gentlemen of the Jury,' said
  The coroner – 'this woman's child
By misadventure met its death.'
  'Aye, aye,' said we. The mother smiled.

And I could see that child's one eye
   Which seemed to laugh, and say with glee:
'What caused my death you'll never know –
   Perhaps my mother murdered me.'

W. H. DAVIES

The Justice of the Peace

Distinguish carefully between these two,
   This thing is yours, that other thing is mine.
You have a shirt, a brimless hat, a shoe
   And half a coat. I am the Lord benign
Of fifty hundred acres of fat land
To which I have a right. You understand?

I have a right because I have, because,
   Because I have – because I have a right.
Now be quite calm and good, obey the laws,
   Remember your low station, do not fight
Against the goad, because, you know, it pricks
Whenever the uncleanly demos kicks.

I do not envy you your hat, your shoe.
   Why should you envy me my small estate?
It's fearfully illogical in you
   To fight with economic force and fate.
Moreover, I have got the upper hand,
And mean to keep it. Do you understand?

HILAIRE BELLOC

Imperial Adam

Imperial Adam, naked in the dew,
  Felt his brown flanks and found the rib had gone.
Puzzled, he turned and saw where, two and two,
  The mighty spoor of Jahweh marked the lawn.

Then he remembered through mysterious sleep
  The surgeon fingers probing at the bone,
The voice so far away, so rich and deep:
  'It is not good for him to live alone'.

Turning once more, he found Man's counterpart
  In tender parody, breathing at his side.
He knew her at first sight; he knew by heart
  Her allegory of sense unsatisfied.

The pawpaw drooped its golden breasts above
  Less generous than the honey of her flesh;
The innocent sunlight showed the place of love;
  The dew on its dark hairs winked crisp and fresh.

This plump gourd severed from his virile root,
  She promised on the turf of Paradise
Delicious pulp of the forbidden fruit;
  Sly as the snake she loosed her sinuous thighs,

And waking, smiled up at him from the grass.
  Her breasts rose softly and he heard her sigh –
From all the beasts, whose pleasant task it was
  In Eden to increase and multiply,

Adam had learned the jolly deed of kind:
    He took her in his arms, and there and then,
Like the clean beasts, embracing from behind,
    Began in joy to found the breed of men.

Then from the spurt of seed within her broke
    Her terrible and triumphant female cry,
Split upward by the sexual lightning stroke.
    It was the beasts now who stood watching by;

The gravid elephant, the calving hind,
    The breeding bitch, the she-ape big with young,
Were the first gentle midwives of mankind:
    The teeming lioness rasped her with her tongue,

The proud vicuna nuzzled her as she slept
    Lax on the grass – and Adam, watching too,
Saw how her dumb breasts in their ripening wept,
    The great pod of her belly swelled and grew,

And saw its water break, and saw, in fear,
    Its quaking muscles in the act of birth,
Between her legs a pigmy face appear –
    And the first murderer lay upon the earth.

A. D. HOPE

At the Railway Station, Upway

'There is not much that I can do,
    For I've no money that's quite my own!'
    Spoke up the pitying child –

A little boy with a violin
At the station before the train came in, –
'But I can play my fiddle to you,
And a nice one 'tis, and good in tone!'

The man in the handcuffs smiled;
The constable looked, and he smiled, too,
    As the fiddle began to twang;
And the man in the handcuffs suddenly sang
            With grimful glee:
            'This life so free
            Is the thing for me!'
And the constable smiled, and said no word,
As if unconscious of what he heard;
And so they went on till the train came in –
The convict, and boy with the violin.

THOMAS HARDY

Homecoming

A Breton returns to his birthplace
After having pulled off several fast deals
He walks in front of the factories at Douarnenez
He recognizes nobody
Nobody recognizes him
He is very sad.
He goes into a *crêpe* shop to eat some *crêpes*
But he can't eat any
There's something that keeps him from swallowing
He pays
He goes out
He lights a cigarette

But he can't smoke it.
There's something
Something in his head
Something bad
He gets sadder and sadder
And suddenly be begins to remember:
Somebody told him when he was little
'You'll end up on the scaffold'
And for years
He never dared do anything
Not even cross the street
Not even go to sea
Nothing absolutely nothing.
He remembers.
The one who'd predicted everything was Uncle Grésillard
Uncle Grésillard who brought everybody bad luck
The swine!
And the Breton thinks of his sister
Who works at Vaugirard,
Of his brother killed in the War
Thinks of all the things he's seen
All the things he's done.
Sadness grips him
He tries again
To light a cigarette
But he doesn't feel like smoking
So then he decides to go see Uncle Grésillard.
He goes
He opens the door
Uncle doesn't recognize him
But he recognizes him
And he says to him:
'Good morning Uncle Grésillard'
And then he wrings his neck

And he ends up on the scaffold at Quimper.
After having eaten two dozen *crêpes*
And smoked a cigarette.

JACQUES PRÉVERT
(*translated by Lawrence Ferlinghetti*)

The Poor Man and the Rich
(on the Sabbath)

The poor man's sins are glaring;
In the face of ghostly warning
  He is caught in the fact
  Of an overt act –
Buying greens on a Sunday morning.

The rich man's sins are hidden,
In the pomp of wealth and station;
  And escape the sight
  Of the children of light,
Who are wise in their generation.

The rich man has a kitchen,
And cooks to dress his dinner;
  The poor who would roast
  To the baker's must post,
And thus become a sinner.

The rich man has a cellar,
And a ready butler by him;
  The poor must steer
  For his pint of beer
Where the saint can't choose but spy him.

The rich man's painted windows
Hide the concerts of the quality;
  The poor can but share
  A crack'd fiddle in the air,
Which offends all sound morality.

The rich man is invisible
In the crowd of his gay society;
  But the poor man's delight
  Is a sore in the sight,
And a stench in the nose of piety.

The rich man has a carriage
Where no rude eye can flout him;
  The poor man's bane
  Is a third-class train,
With the daylight all about him.

The rich man goes out yachting,
Where sanctity can't pursue him;
  The poor goes afloat
  In a fourpenny boat,
Where the bishop groans to view him.

T. L. PEACOCK

The Entranced

Seen black against the fog and snow,
Close by the big vent-hole, whose glow
  Is warm and red,

With rounded bottoms crouch – heart breaking! –
Five children, eyes on the man baking
  Pale, heavy bread.

They watch the strong white arm that plies
The greyish dough, till soon it lies
  In its bright lair.

They hear the good bread hissing, while
The baker with a cosy smile
  Hums an old air.

They huddle near, and not one stirs
As the red vent-hole breathes and purrs,
  Warm as a breast.

When, ordered for some midnight rout,
In crescent shapes the bread comes out,
  How keen their zest!

And when, beneath the smoky beams,
The perfumed crust so sweetly screams,
  And crickets chatter,

What breath of life comes through the hole!
It penetrates them to the soul
  Through every tatter.

They're having such a lovely time,
Poor little Christs all stiff with rime,
  Just to be there,

Nuzzling the bars, with mutterings
Of wonder at these lovely things
  In the oven's glare;

Quite stupid, bent in adoration
Before this brilliant revelation
  Of heaven grown kind,

Bent down so low, their breeches crack
And shirts fly loose from each small back
  In the cold wind.

ARTHUR RIMBAUD
(*translated by Norman Cameron*)

Lazy Morning

It's terrible
the faint sound
of a hardboiled egg cracked on a tin counter
it's terrible this noise
when it stirs in the memory of a man who's hungry
also terrible is the head of the man
the head of the man who's hungry
when he looks at himself at six in the morning
in the mirror of a big store
a head the colour of dust
it's not his head however which he looks at
in the window of *Chez Potin*
he doesn't give a damn for his head
he doesn't think of it
he dreams
he imagines another head
a calf's head for instance
with vinegar sauce
or a head of no matter what that's edible
and he moves his jaw gently

gently
and he grinds his teeth gently
because the world pays for its head
and he can't do anything against this world
and he counts on his fingers one two three
one two three
that makes three days he hasn't eaten
useless to repeat to himself Three Days
It can't last
it lasts
three days
three nights
without eating
and behind these windowpanes
patés bottles preserves
dead fish protected by their cans
cans protected by windowpanes
windowpanes protected by cops
cops protected by fear
what barricades for six unhappy sardines . . .

A little further on the Café
coffee with cream and hot rolls
the man staggers
and inside his head
a fog of words
A haze of words
sardines to eat
hardboiled egg coffee with cream
coffee watered with rum
coffee with cream
coffee with cream
coffee with crime watered with blood . . .
A man highly esteemed in his neighbourhood

has had his throat cut in full daylight
the assassin the bum stole two francs
from him
or one watered coffee
zero francs sixtyfive centimes
two pieces of bread and butter
and twentyfive centimes for the tip

It's terrible
the faint sound of a hardboiled egg
cracked on a tin counter
it's terrible this noise
when it stirs in the memory
of a man who's hungry

JACQUES PRÉVERT
(*translated by Lawrence Ferlinghetti*)

A Death Song

What cometh here from west to east awending?
And who are these, the marchers stern and slow?
We bear the message that the rich are sending
Aback to those who bade them wake and know.
Not one, not one, nor thousands must they slay,
But one and all if they would dusk the day.

We asked them for a life of toilsome earning,
They bade us bide their leisure for our bread;
We craved to speak to tell our woeful learning:
We come back speechless, bearing back our dead.
Not one, not one, nor thousands must they slay,
But one and all if they would dusk the day.

They will not learn; they have no ears to hearken.
They turn their faces from the eyes of fate;
Their gay-lit halls shut out the skies that darken.
But, lo! this dead man knocking at the gate.
Not one, not one, nor thousands must they slay,
But one and all if they would dusk the day.

Here lies the sign that we shall break our prison;
Amidst the storm he won a prisoner's rest;
But in the cloudy dawn the sun arisen
Brings us our day of work to win the best.
Not one, not one, nor thousands must they slay,
But one and all if they would dusk the day.

WILLIAM MORRIS

Danny

One night a score of Erris men,
A score I'm told and nine,
Said, 'We'll get shut of Danny's noise
Of girls and widows dyin'.

'There's not his like from Binghamstown
To Boyle and Ballycroy,
At playing hell on decent girls,
At beating man and boy.

'He's left two pairs of female twins
Beyond in Killacreest,
And twice in Crossmolina fair
He's struck the parish priest.

151

'But we'll come round him in the night
A mile beyond the Mullet;
Ten will quench his bloody eyes,
And ten will choke his gullet.'

It wasn't long till Danny came,
From Bangor making way,
And he was damning moon and stars
And whistling grand and gay.

Till in a gap of hazel glen –
And not a hare in sight –
Out lepped the nine-and-twenty lads
Along his left and right.

Then Danny smashed the nose on Byrne,
He split the lips on three,
And bit across the right hand thumb
Of one Red Shawn Magee.

But seven tripped him up behind,
And seven kicked before,
And seven squeezed around his throat
Till Danny kicked no more.

Then some destroyed him with their heels,
Some tramped him in the mud,
Some stole his purse and timber pipe,
And some washed off his blood.

.   .   .   .

And when you're walking out the way
From Bangor to Belmullet,
You'll see a flat cross on a stone
Where men choked Danny's gullet.

J. M. SYNGE

Send No Money

Standing under the fobbed
Impendent belly of Time
Tell me the truth, I said,
Teach me the way things go.
All the other lads there
Were itching to have a bash,
But I thought waiting unfair:
It and finding out clash.

So he patted my head, booming *Boy,*
There's no green in your eye:
Sit here, and watch the hail
Of occurrence clobber life out
To a shape no one sees –
Dare you look at that straight?
Oh thank you, I said, *Oh yes please,*
And sat down to wait.

Half life is over now,
And I meet full face on dark mornings
The bestial visor, bent in
By the blows of what happened to happen.
What does it prove? Sod all.
In this way I spent youth,
Tracing the trite untransferable
Truss-advertisement, truth.

PHILIP LARKIN

Lausanne

In Gibbon's Old Garden: 11–12 p.m., *June 27, 1897*

The 110th anniversary of the completion of the 'Decline and Fall' at the same hour and place.

A spirit seems to pass,
Formal in pose, but grave withal and grand:
He contemplates a volume in his hand,
And far lamps fleck him through the thin acacias.

Anon the book is closed,
With 'It is finished!' And at the alley's end
He turns, and when on me his glances bend
As from the Past comes speech – small, muted, yet composed.

'How fares the Truth now? – Ill?
– Do pens but slily further her advance?
May one not speed her but in phrase askance?
Do scribes aver the Comic to be Reverend still?

'Still rule those minds on earth
At whom sage Milton's wormwood words were hurled:
"*Truth like a bastard comes into the world
Never without ill-fame to him who gives her birth*"?'

THOMAS HARDY

The Lie

Go, soul, the body's guest,
　Upon a thankless arrant;
Fear not to touch the best;
　The truth shall be thy warrant.
　　Go, since I needs must die,
　　And give the world the lie.

Say to the court, it glows
  And shines like rotten wood;
Say to the church, it shows
  What's good, and doth no good:
    If church and court reply,
    Then give them both the lie.

Tell potentates, they live
  Acting by others' action,
Not loved unless they give,
  Not strong but by their faction:
    If potentates reply,
    Give potentates the lie.

Tell men of high condition
  That manage the estate,
Their purpose is ambition,
  Their practice only hate:
    And if they once reply,
    Then give them all the lie.

Tell them that brave it most,
  They beg for more by spending,
Who, in their greatest cost,
  Seek nothing but commending:
    And if they make reply,
    Then give them all the lie.

Tell zeal it wants devotion;
  Tell love it is but lust;
Tell time it is but motion;
  Tell flesh it is but dust:
    And wish them not reply,
    For thou must give the lie.

Tell age it daily wasteth;
　Tell honour how it alters;
Tell beauty how she blasteth;
　Tell favour how it falters:
　　And as they shall reply,
　　Give every one the lie.

Tell wit how much it wrangles
　In tickle points of niceness;
Tell wisdom she entangles
　Herself in over-wiseness:
　　And when they do reply,
　　Straight give them both the lie.

Tell physic of her boldness;
　Tell skill it is prevention;
Tell charity of coldness;
　Tell law it is contention:
　　And as they do reply,
　　So give them still the lie.

Tell fortune of her blindness;
　Tell nature of decay;
Tell friendship of unkindness;
　Tell justice of delay:
　　And if they will reply,
　　Then give them all the lie.

Tell arts they have no soundness,
　But vary by esteeming;
Tell schools they want profoundness,
　And stand too much on seeming:
　　If arts and schools reply,
　　Give arts and schools the lie.

Tell faith it 's fled the city;
   Tell how the country erreth;
Tell, manhood shakes off pity;
   Tell, virtue least preferreth:
      And if they do reply,
      Spare not to give the lie.

So when thou hast, as I
   Commanded thee, done blabbing,
Although to give the lie
   Deserves no less than stabbing,
      Stab at thee he that will,
      No stab the soul can kill.

SIR WALTER RALEGH

Hard Times

Be forewarned you old guys
be forewarned you heads of families
the time when you gave your sons to the country
as one gives bread to pigeons
that time won't come again
resign yourself to it
it's over
cherry time won't come again
nor the time of cherry stones
useless to moan about it
go to sleep instead
you're falling asleep
your shroud is freshly pressed
the sandman is coming
adjust your chin-straps

157

close the eyelids
the sludge-collector's coming to carry you away
it's over the three musketeers
now's the sewerman's time

The time when with a big smile in the subway
you asked us politely
two dots open quotes
are you getting off at the next stop
young man
it was the war you were talking about
but you won't be giving us the fatherly patriotic treatment
   anymore
no my captain
no Mister Such and Such
no papa
no mama
we're not getting off at the next stop
unless we put you off ahead of us
we'll throw you out the door
it's more practical than the graveyard
it's gayer
quicker
cheaper

Whenever you drew straws
it was always the ship's boy you dined upon
but the time of joyous sinkings is past
when admirals fall at sea
don't count on us to throw them the lifebuoy
at least unless it's made of stone
or of flatiron
resign yourself to it
the time of the old old men is over

The time when you came back from the dress parade
with your children on your shoulders
you were drunk without having drunk anything
and your spinal cord
pranced with pride and joy
in front of the army barracks
your head went haywire
when the handsome horse-guards passed
and the military music
tickled you from head to toe
tickled you
and the kids you carried on your shoulders
you let them slide off into the tricoloured mud
into the clay of the dead
and your shoulders became bowed
youth must pass by
you let it die

Honourable and highly respected men
in your neighbourhood
you meet each other
you congratulate each other
you clot together
alas alas dear Mister Babylas
I had three sons and I gave them
to the country
alas alas dear Mister of my two
me I gave only two
one does what one can
what do they expect of us
do you still have pain in the knees
and a tear in the eye
the false snot of mourning

a black band on the hat
feet nice and warm
funeral wreathes
and the garlic in the mutton
you remember before the War
the absinthe spoons the horse carriages
the hairpins
the torchlight Retreats
ah how wonderful it was
those were the good old days

Shut up greybeard
stop running your dead tongue
between your false ivory teeth
the time of hair carriages
the time of horse pins
that time won't come again
right by fours
muster your old bones
the paddywagon
the hearse of the rich is coming
sons of Saint Louis rise up to heaven
the performance is over
this whole pretty world will get together again up there
near the Good Lord of Cops
in the yard of the Hall of Justice

To the rear grandfather
to the rear father and mother
to the rear grandfathers
to the rear Old Soldiers
to the rear old chaplains
to the rear old bags

the performance is over
now for the kids
the show's about to begin

JACQUES PRÉVERT
(*translated by Lawrence Ferlinghetti*)

The Laws of God, the Laws of Man

The laws of God, the laws of man,
He may keep that will and can;
Not I: let God and man decree
Laws for themselves and not for me;
And if my ways are not as theirs
Let them mind their own affairs.
Their deeds I judge and much condemn,
Yet when did I make laws for them?
Please yourselves, say I, and they
Need only look the other way.
But no, they will not; they must still
Wrest their neighbour to their will,
And make me dance as they desire
With jail and gallows and hell-fire.
And how am I to face the odds
Of man's bedevilment and God's?
I, a stranger and afraid
In a world I never made.
They will be master, right or wrong;
Though both are foolish, both are strong.
And since, my soul, we cannot fly
To Saturn nor to Mercury,
Keep we must, if keep we can,
These foreign laws of God and man.

A. E. HOUSMAN

161

He, standing hushed, a pace or two apart,
    Among the bluebells of the listless plain,
Thinks, and remembers how he cleansed his heart
    And washed his hands in innocence in vain.

A. E. HOUSMAN

THIS LIFE, AND HOW WE LIVE IT

Inscription above the Entrance
to the Abbey of Theleme

Here enter not vile bigots, hypocrites,
Externally devoted Apes, base snites,
Puft up, wry-necked beasts, worse than the Huns
Or Ostrogots, forerunners of baboons:
Curst snakes, dissembled varlets, seeming Sancts,
Slipshod caffards, beggars pretending wants,
Fat chuff-cats, smell-feast knockers, doltish gulls,
Out-strouting cluster-fists, contentious bulls,
Fomenters of divisions and debates,
Elsewhere, not here, make sale of your deceits.

   Your filthy trumperies
   Stuff't with pernicious lies,
     (Not worth a bubble)
     Would do but trouble
   Our earthly Paradise,
   Your filthy trumperies.

Here enter not Attorneys, Barristers,
Nor bridle-champing law-Practitioners:
Clerks, Commissaries, Scribes nor Pharisees,
Wilful disturbers of the People's ease:
Judges, destroyers, with an unjust breath,
Of honest men, like dogs, ev'n unto death.
Your salary is at the gibbet-foot:
Go drink there; for we do not here fly out
On those excessive courses, which may draw
A waiting on your courts by suits in law.

Lawsuits, debates and wrangling
Hence are exil'd, and jangling
  Here we are very
  Frolick and merry,
And free from all entangling,
Lawsuits, debates and wrangling.

Here enter not base pinching Usurers,
Pelf-lickers, everlasting gatherers.
Gold-graspers, coin-gripers, gulpers of mists:
Niggish deformed sots, who, though your chests
Vast sums of money should to you afford,
Would ne'er the less add more unto that hoard,
And yet be not content, you cluntchfist dastards,
Insatiable fiends, and Pluto's bastards.
Greedy devourers, chichie sneakbill rogues,
Hell-mastiffs gnaw your bones, you rav'nous dogs.

  You beastly looking fellows,
  Reason doth plainly tell us,
    That we should not
    To you allot
  Room here, but at the gallows,
  You beastly looking fellows.

Here enter not fond makers of demurs
In love adventures, peevish, jealous curs.
Sad pensive dotards, raisers of garboils,
Hags, goblins, ghosts, firebrands of household broils.
Nor drunkards, liars, cowards, cheaters, clowns,
Thieves, cannibals, faces o'ercast with frowns.
Nor lazy slugs, envious, covetous:
Nor blockish, cruel, nor too credulous.
Here mangy, pocky folks shall have no place,
No ugly lusks, nor persons of disgrace.

166

Grace, honour, praise, delight,
Here sojourn day and night.
　　Sound bodies lin'd
　　With a good mind,
Do here pursue with might
Grace, honour, praise, delight.

Here enter you, and welcome from our hearts,
All noble sparks, endow'd with gallant parts.
This is the glorious place, which bravely shall
Afford wherewith to entertain you all.
Were you a thousand, here you shall not want
For any thing; for what you'll ask, we'll grant.
Stay here, you lively, jovial, handsome, brisk,
Gay, witty, frolic, cheerful, merry, frisk,
Spruce, jocund, courteous, furtherers of trades,
And, in a word, all worthy gentile blades.

　　Blades of heroic breasts
　　Shall taste here of the feasts,
　　　　Both privily
　　　　And civily
　　Of the celestial guests,
　　Blades of heroic breasts.

Here enter you, pure, honest, faithful, true,
Expounders of the Scriptures old and new.
Whose glosses do not blind our reason, but
Make it to see the clearer, and who shut
Its passages from hatred, avarice,
Pride, factions, cov'nants, and all sort of vice.
Come, settle here a charitable faith,
Which neighbourly affection nourisheth.
And whose light chaseth all corrupters hence,
Of the blest Word, from the aforesaid sense.

The Holy Sacred Word
May it always afford
　　T'us all in common
　　Both man and woman
A sp'ritual shield and sword,
The Holy Sacred Word.

Here enter you all Ladies of high birth,
Delicious, stately, charming, full of mirth,
Ingenious, lovely, miniard, proper, fair,
Magnetic, graceful, splendid, pleasant, rare,
Obliging, sprightly, virtuous, young, solacious,
Kind, neat, quick, feat, bright, compt, ripe, choice, dear,
　　　　precious.
Alluring, courtly, comely, fine, complete,
Wise, personable, ravishing and sweet.
Come joys enjoy, the Lord Celestial
Hath giv'n enough, wherewith to please us all.

Gold give us, God forgive us,
And from all woes relieve us.
　　That we the treasure
　　May reap of pleasure.
And shun what e'er is grievous.
Gold give us, God forgive us.

FRANÇOIS RABELAIS
(<i>translated by Sir Thomas Urquhart</i>)

Walt Whitman, a Kosmos

(from *Song of Myself*)

Walt Whitman, a kosmos, of Manhattan the son,
Turbulent, fleshy, sensual, eating, drinking and breeding,
No sentimentalist, no stander above men and women or apart
    from them,
No more modest than immodest.

Unscrew the locks from the doors!
Unscrew the doors themselves from their jambs!

Whoever degrades another degrades me,
And whatever is done or said returns at last to me.

Through me the afflatus surging and surging, through me the
    current and index.

I speak the pass-word primeval, I give the sign of democracy,
By God! I will accept nothing which all cannot have their
    counterpart of on the same terms.

Through me many long dumb voices,
Voices of the interminable generation of prisoners and slaves,
Voices of the diseas'd and despairing and of thieves and
    dwarfs,
Voices of cycles of preparation and accretion,
And of the threads that connect the stars, and of wombs and
    of the father-stuff,
And of the rights of them the others are down upon,
Of the deform'd, trivial, flat, foolish, despised,
Fog in the air, beetles rolling balls of dung.

Through me forbidden voices,
Voices of sexes and lusts, voices veil'd and I remove the veil,
Voices indecent by me clarified and transfigur'd.

I do not press my fingers across my mouth,
I keep as delicate around the bowels as around the head and
    heart,
Copulation is no more rank to me than death is.

I believe in the flesh and the appetites,
Seeing, hearing, feeling, are miracles, and each part and tag of
    me is a miracle.
Divine am I inside and out, and I make holy whatever I touch
    or am touch'd from,
The scent of these arm-pits aroma finer than prayer,
This head more than churches, bibles, and all the creeds.

If I worship one thing more than another it shall be the spread
    of my own body, or any part of it,
Translucent mould of me it shall be you!
Shaded ledges and rests it shall be you!
Firm masculine colter it shall be you!
Whatever goes to the tilth of me it shall be you!
You my rich blood! your milky stream pale strippings of my
    life!
Breast that presses against other breasts it shall be you!
My brain it shall be your occult convolutions!
Root of wash'd sweet-flag! timorous pond-snipe! nest of
    guarded duplicate eggs! it shall be you!
Mix'd tussled hay of head, beard, brawn, it shall be you!
Trickling sap of maple, fibre of manly wheat, it shall be you!
Sun so generous it shall be you!
Vapors lighting and shading my face it shall be you!
You sweaty brooks and dews it shall be you!

Winds whose soft-tickling genitals rub against me it shall be
    you!
Broad muscular fields, branches of live oak, loving lounger in
    my winding paths, it shall be you!
Hands I have taken, face I have kiss'd, mortal I have ever
    touch'd, it shall be you.

I dote on myself, there is that lot of me and all so luscious,
Each moment and whatever happens thrills me with joy,
I cannot tell how my ankles bend, nor whence the cause of my
    faintest wish,
Nor the cause of the friendship I emit, nor the cause of the
    friendship I take again.

That I walk up my stoop, I pause to consider if it really be,
A morning-glory at my window satisfies me more than the
    metaphysics of books.
To behold the day-break!
The little light fades the immense and diaphanous shadows,
The air tastes good to my palate.

Hefts of the moving world at innocent gambols silently rising,
    freshly exuding,
Scooting obliquely high and low.

Something I cannot see puts upward libidinous prongs,
Seas of bright juice suffuse heaven.

The earth by the sky staid with, the daily close of their junction,
The heav'd challenge from the east that moment over my
    head,
The mocking taunt, See then whether you shall be master!

WALT WHITMAN

A Supermarket in California

What thoughts I have of you tonight, Walt Whitman, for I walked down the sidestreets under the trees with a headache self-conscious looking at the full moon.

In my hungry fatigue, and shopping for images, I went into the neon fruit supermarket, dreaming of your enumerations!

What peaches and what penumbras! Whole families shopping at night! Aisles full of husbands! Wives in the avocados, babies in the tomatoes! – and you, Garcia Lorca, what were you doing down by the watermelons?

I saw you, Walt Whitman, childless, lonely old grubber, poking among the meats in the refrigerator and eyeing the grocery boys.

I heard you asking questions of each: Who killed the pork chops? What price bananas? Are you my Angel?

I wandered in and out of the brilliant stacks of cans following you, and followed in my imagination by the store detective.

We strode down the open corridors together in our solitary fancy tasting artichokes, possessing every frozen delicacy, and never passing the cashier.

Where are we going, Walt Whitman? The doors close in an hour. Which way does your beard point tonight?

(I touch your book and dream of our odyssey in the supermarket and feel absurd.)

Will we walk all night through solitary streets? The trees add shade to shade, lights out in the houses, we'll both be lonely.

Will we stroll dreaming of the lost America of love past blue automobiles in driveways, home to our silent cottage?

Ah, dear father, graybeard, lonely old courage-teacher,

what America did you have when Charon quit poling his ferry
and you got out on a smoking bank and stood watching the
boat disappear on the black waters of Lethe?

Berkeley 1955

ALLEN GINSBERG

The Australian Poem

A sunburnt bloody stockman stood,
And in a dismal bloody mood
Apostrophized his bloody cuddy:
'This bloody moke's no bloody good,
He doesn't earn his bloody food,
Bloody, bloody, bloody.'

He leapt upon his bloody horse
And galloped off of bloody course.
The road was wet and bloody muddy,
It led him to the bloody creek.
The bloody horse was bloody weak.
Bloody, bloody, bloody.

He said 'This bloody steed must swim,
The same for me as bloody him.'
The creek was deep and bloody floody,
So ere they reached the bloody bank
The bloody steed beneath him sank,
The stockman's face a bloody study,
Ejaculating bloody, bloody, bloody.

ANONYMOUS

Spleen

I'm like the King of some damp, rainy clime,
Grown impotent and old before my time,
Who scorns the bows and scrapings of his teachers
And bores himself with hounds and all such creatures.
Naught can amuse him, falcon, steed, or chase:
No, not the mortal plight of his whole race
Dying before his balcony. The tune,
Sung to this tyrant by his pet buffoon,
Irks him. His couch seems far more like a grave.
Even the girls, for whom all kings seem brave,
Can think no toilet up, nor shameless rig,
To draw a smirk from this funereal prig.
The sage who makes him gold, could never find
The baser element that rots his mind.
Even those blood-baths the old Romans knew
And later thugs have imitated too,
Can't warm this skeleton to deeds of slaughter,
Whose only blood is Lethe's cold, green water.

CHARLES BAUDELAIRE
(*translated by Roy Campbell*)

Epigram

I ran upon life unknowing, without or science or art,
I found the first pretty maiden but she was a harlot at heart;
I wandered about the woodland after the melting of snow,
'Here is the first pretty snowdrop' – and it was the dung of
a crow!

ALFRED TENNYSON

To the Reader

Folly and error, avarice and vice,
Employ our souls and waste our bodies' force.
As mangy beggars incubate their lice,
We nourish our innocuous remorse.

Our sins are stubborn, craven our repentance.
For our weak vows we ask excessive prices.
Trusting our tears will wash away the sentence,
We sneak off where the muddy road entices.

Cradled in evil, that Thrice-Great Magician,
The Devil, rocks our souls, that can't resist;
And the rich metal of our own volition
Is vaporized by that sage alchemist.

The Devil pulls the strings by which we're worked:
By all revolting objects lured, we slink
Hellwards; each day down one more step we're jerked
Feeling no horror, through the shades that stink.

Just as a lustful pauper bites and kisses
The scarred and shrivelled breast of an old whore,
We steal, along the roadside, furtive blisses,
Squeezing them, like stale oranges, for more.

Packed tight, like hives of maggots, thickly seething,
Within our brains a host of demons surges.
Deep down into our lungs at every breathing,
Death flows, an unseen river, moaning dirges.

If rape or arson, poison, or the knife
Has wove no pleasing patterns in the stuff
Of this drab canvas we accept as life –
It is because we are not bold enough!

Amongst the jackals, leopards, mongrels, apes,
Snakes, scorpions, vultures, that with hellish din,
Squeal, roar, writhe, gambol, crawl, with monstrous shapes,
In each man's foul menagerie of sin –

There's one more damned than all. He never gambols,
Nor crawls, nor roars, but, from the rest withdrawn,
Gladly of this whole earth would make a shambles
And swallow up existence with a yawn . . .

Boredom! He smokes his hookah, while he dreams
Of gibbets, weeping tears he cannot smother.
You know this dainty monster, too, it seems –
Hypocrite reader! – You! – My twin! – My brother!

CHARLES BAUDELAIRE
(*translated by Roy Campbell*)

Ballade

(Against Envious Tongues)

In arsenic, realgar triturate;
In quicklime and saltpetre; in a froth
Of boiling lead, where let them macerate;
In soot and pitch left soaking in a broth
Of urine from a ghetto's public booth;
In rinsings from a leper's mangy poll;
In scrapings from a patten's crusted sole;
In philtres venomous; in viper's blood;
In gall of fox and wolf and eldritch owl,
Let all such envious tongues as these be stew'd!

In brains of an old hydrophobic cat,
Grimalkin who hath neither claw nor tooth,
Or of a mastiff so infuriate
That slobber overflows his baying mouth;
In flecks of spume, congeal'd by dust and drouth
Upon the flanks of a wind-broken mule;
In water where the rat hath dipp'd its jowl,
Together with the slimy snake and toad,
Lizard and frog and other noble fowl,
Let all such envious tongues as these be stew'd!

In dangerous corrosive sublimate;
In navel torn from serpent still in youth;
In blood left drying on a surgeon's plate
When a full moon ascends the azimuth
(Blood either black, or green as leeks, or both);
In chancres and in ulcers; in a bowl
Wherein a nurse has wash'd her baby's tow'l;
In basin where a trull has shed her load
(He whom this puzzles is a simple soul),
Let all such envious tongues as these be stew'd!

Prince, take this dainty dish and sift the whole
(If you have neither sieve nor sack nor shroud)
Through dirty draw'rs with grease and sweat imbued;
But, first, in a fat porker's filthy stool
Let all such envious tongues as these be stew'd!

FRANÇOIS VILLON
(*translated by Norman Cameron*)

Miniver Cheevy

Miniver Cheevy, child of scorn,
   Grew lean while he assailed the seasons;
He wept that he was ever born,
   And he had reasons.

Miniver loved the days of old
   When swords were bright and steeds were prancing;
The vision of a warrior bold
   Would set him dancing.

Miniver sighed for what was not,
   And dreamed, and rested from his labors;
He dreamed of Thebes and Camelot,
   And Priam's neighbors.

Miniver mourned the ripe renown
   That made so many a name so fragrant;
He mourned Romance, now on the town,
   And Art, a vagrant.

Miniver loved the Medici,
   Albeit he had never seen one;
He would have sinned incessantly
   Could he have been one.

Miniver cursed the commonplace
   And eyed a khaki suit with loathing;
He missed the medieval grace
   Of iron clothing.

Miniver scorned the gold he sought,
   But sore annoyed was he without it;
Miniver thought, and thought, and thought,
   And thought about it.

Miniver Cheevy, born too late,
  Scratched his head and kept on thinking;
Miniver coughed, and called it fate,
  And kept on drinking.

EDWIN ARLINGTON ROBINSON

An Epitaph

Stet quicunque volet potens
Aulæ culmine lubrico, &c.   Senec.

INTERR'D beneath this Marble Stone,
Lie Saunt'ring JACK, and Idle JOAN.
While rolling Threescore Years and One
Did round this Globe their Courses run;
If Human Things went Ill or Well;
If changing Empires rose or fell;
The Morning past, the Evening came,
And found this Couple still the same.
They Walk'd and Eat, good Folks: What then?
Why then They Walk'd and Eat again:
They soundly slept the Night away:
They did just Nothing all the Day;
And having bury'd Children Four,
Wou'd not take Pains to try for more.
Nor Sister either had, nor Brother:
They seem'd just Tally'd for each other.
  Their Moral and Oeconomy
Most perfectly They made agree:
Each Virtue kept its proper Bound,
Nor Trespass'd on the other's Ground.
Nor Fame, nor Censure They regarded:
They neither Punish'd, nor Rewarded.

He car'd not what the Footmen did:
Her Maids She neither prais'd, nor chid:
So ev'ry Servant took his Course;
And bad at First, They all grew worse.
Slothful Disorder fill'd His Stable;
And sluttish Plenty deck'd Her Table.
Their Beer was strong; Their Wine was *Port*;
Their Meal was large; Their Grace was short.
They gave the Poor the Remnant-meat,
Just when it grew not fit to eat.

They paid the Church and Parish-Rate;
And took, but read not the Receit:
For which They claim'd their *Sunday*'s Due,
Of slumb'ring in an upper Pew.

No Man's Defects sought They to know;
So never made Themselves a Foe.
No Man's good Deeds did They commend;
So never rais'd Themselves a Friend.
Nor cherish'd They Relations poor:
That might decrease Their present Store:
Nor Barn nor House did they repair:
That might oblige Their future Heir.

They neither Added, nor Confounded:
They neither Wanted, nor Abounded.
Each *Christmas* They Accompts did clear;
And wound their Bottom round the Year.
Nor Tear, nor Smile did They imploy
At News of Public Grief, or Joy.
When Bells were Rung, and Bonfires made;
If ask'd, They ne'er deny'd their Aid:
Their Jugg was to the Ringers carry'd;
Who ever either Dy'd, or Marry'd.
Their Billet at the Fire was found;
Who ever was Depos'd, or Crown'd.

Nor Good, nor Bad, nor Fools, nor Wise;
They wou'd not learn, nor cou'd advise:
Without Love, Hatred, Joy, or Fear,
They led – a kind of – as it were:
Nor Wish'd, nor Car'd, nor Laugh'd, nor Cry'd:
And so They liv'd; and so They dy'd.

MATTHEW PRIOR

Holy Willie's Prayer

And send the Godly in a pet to pray—POPE

Argument

Holy Willie was a rather oldish bachelor Elder in the parish of Mauch-
line, and much and justly famed for that polemical chattering which
ends in tippling Orthodoxy, and for that Spiritualized Bawdry which
refines to Liquorish Devotion. – In a Sessional process with a gentleman
in Mauchline, a Mr Gavin Hamilton, Holy Willie, and his priest, father
Auld, after full hearing in the Presbytery of Ayr, came off but second
best; owing partly to the oratorical powers of Mr Robert Aiken, Mr
Hamilton's Counsel; but chiefly to Mr Hamilton's being one of the most
irreproachable and truly respectable characters in the country. – On
losing his Process, the Muse overheard him at his devotions as follows –

O thou that in the heavens does dwell!
Wha, as it pleases best thysel,
Sends ane to heaven and ten to hell,
        A' for thy glory!
And no for ony gude or ill
        They've done before thee.

I bless and praise thy matchless might,
When thousands thou has left in night,
That I am here before thy sight,

For gifts and grace,
A burning and a shining light
To a' this place.

What was I, or my generation,
That I should get such exaltation?
I, wha deserv'd most just damnation,
For broken laws
Sax thousand years ere my creation,
Thro' Adam's cause!

When from my mother's womb I fell,
Thou might hae plunged me deep in hell,
To gnash my gooms, and weep, and wail,
In burning lakes,
Where damned devils roar and yell
Chain'd to their stakes.

Yet I am here, a chosen sample,
To shew thy grace is great and ample:
I'm here, a pillar o' thy temple
Strong as a rock,
A guide, a ruler and example
To a' thy flock.

But yet – O Lord – confess I must –
At times I'm fash'd wi' fleshly lust;
And sometimes too, in warldly trust
Vile Self gets in;
But thou remembers we are dust,
Defil'd wi' sin.

fash'd bothered

182

O Lord – yestreen – thou kens – wi' Meg –
Thy pardon I sincerely beg!
O may 't ne'er be a living plague,
      To my dishonour!
And I'll ne'er lift a lawless leg
      Again upon her.

Besides, I farther maun avow,
Wi' Leezie's lass, three times – I trow –
But Lord, that Friday I was fou
      When I cam near her;
Or else, thou kens, thy servant true
      Wad never steer her.

Maybe thou lets this fleshy thorn
Buffet thy servant e'en and morn,
Lest he o'er proud and high should turn,
      That he 's sae gifted;
If sae, thy hand maun e'en be borne
      Untill thou lift it.

Lord bless thy Chosen in this place,
For here thou has a chosen race:
But God, confound their stubborn face,
      And blast their name,
Wha bring thy rulers to disgrace
      And open shame.

Lord mind Gaun Hamilton's deserts!
He drinks, and swears, and plays at cartes,
Yet has sae mony taking arts
      Wi' Great and Sma',
Frae God's ain priest the people's hearts
      He steals awa.

steer meddle with

And when we chasten'd him therefore,
Thou kens how he bred sic a splore,
And set the warld in a roar
      O' laughin at us:
Curse thou his basket and his store,
        Kail and potatoes.

Lord hear my earnest cry and prayer
Against that Presbytry of Ayr!
Thy strong right hand, Lord, make it bare
      Upon their heads!
Lord visit them, and dinna spare,
        For their misdeeds!

O Lord my God, that glib-tongu'd Aiken!
My very heart and flesh are quaking
To think how I sat, sweating, shaking,
      And piss'd wi' dread,
While Auld wi' hingin lip gaed sneaking
      And hid his head!

Lord, in thy day o' vengeance try him!
Lord visit him that did employ him!
And pass not in thy mercy by them,
      Nor hear their prayer;
But for thy people's sake destroy them,
      And dinna spare!

But Lord, remember me and mine
Wi' mercies temporal and divine!

splore fuss
hingin hanging

That I for grace and gear may shine,
    Excell'd by nane!
And a' the glory shall be thine!
    AMEN! AMEN!

ROBERT BURNS

On Mundane Acquaintances

Good morning, Algernon: Good morning, Percy.
Good morning, Mrs Roebeck. Christ have mercy!

HILAIRE BELLOC

Aunt Jane

'Mamma' said Amanda 'I want to know what
    Our relatives mean when they say
That Aunt Jane is a Gorgon who ought to be shot,
    Or at any rate taken away.

'Pray what is a Gorgon and why do you shoot
    It? Or are its advances refused?
Or is it perhaps a maleficent Brute?
    I protest I am wholly bemused.'

'The Term,' said her Mother, 'is certain to pain,
    And is quite inexcusably rude.
Moreover Aunt Jane, though uncommonly plain,
    Is also uncommonly good.

gear wealth

'She provides information without hesitation.
  For people unwilling to learn;
And often bestows good advice upon those
  Who give her no thanks in return.

'She is down before anyone's up in the place –
  That is, up before anyone's down.
Her Domestics are awed by the shape of her face
  And they tremble with fear at her frown.

'Her visiting list is of Clergymen who
  Have reached a respectable age,
And she pays her companion Miss Angela Drew
  A sufficient and regular wage.

'Her fortune is large, though we often remark
  On a modesty rare in the rich;
For her nearest and dearest are quite in the dark
  As to what she will leave, or to which.

'Her conduct has ever been totally free
  From censorious whispers of ill,
At any rate, since 1903 –
  And probably earlier still.

'Your Father's dear sister presents, in a word,
  A model for all of her sex,
With a firmness of will that is never deterred,
  And a confidence nothing can vex.

'I can only desire that you too should aspire
  To such earthly reward as appears
In a high reputation, at present entire,
  After Heaven knows how many years.

HILAIRE BELLOC · SIR WALTER RALEIGH

'So in future remember to turn a deaf ear
  To detraction – and now run away
To your brothers and sisters whose laughter I hear
  In the garden below us at play.'

'Oh thank you, Mamma!' said Amanda at that,
  And ran off to the innocent band
Who were merrily burying Thomas the Cat
  Right up to his neck in the sand.

HILAIRE BELLOC

Wishes of an Elderly Man

I wish I loved the Human Race;
I wish I loved its silly face;
I wish I liked the way it walks;
I wish I liked the way it talks;
And when I'm introduced to one
I wish I thought *What Jolly Fun!*

SIR WALTER RALEIGH

At a Country Fair

At a bygone Western country fair
I saw a giant led by a dwarf
With a red string like a long thin scarf;
How much he was the stronger there
  The giant seemed unaware.

187

And then I saw that the giant was blind,
And the dwarf a shrewd-eyed little thing;
The giant, mild, timid, obeyed the string
As if he had no independent mind,
　　Or will of any kind.

Wherever the dwarf decided to go
At his heels the other trotted meekly,
(Perhaps – I know not – reproaching weakly)
Like one Fate bade that it must be so,
　　Whether he wished or no.

Various sights in various climes
I have seen, and more I may see yet,
But that sight never shall I forget,
And have thought it the sorriest of pantomimes,
　　If once, a hundred times!

THOMAS HARDY

What, After All, Are All Things – But a Show?
(from *Don Juan*)

O Love! O Glory! What are you who fly
　　Around us ever, rarely to alight?
There's not a meteor in the Polar sky
　　Of such transcendent and more fleeting flight.
Chill, and chain'd to cold earth, we lift on high
　　Our eyes in search of either lovely light;
A thousand and a thousand colours they
Assume, then leave us on our freezing way.

And such as they are, such my present tale is,
  A nondescript and ever-varying rhyme,
A versified Aurora Borealis,
  Which flashes o'er a waste and icy clime.
When we know what all are, we must bewail us,
  But ne'ertheless I hope it is no crime
To laugh at *all* things – for I wish to know
What, after *all*, are *all* things – but a *show?*

They accuse me – *Me* – the present writer of
  The present poem – of – I know not what –
A tendency to under-rate and scoff
  At human power and virtue, and all that;
And this they say in language rather rough.
  Good God! I wonder what they would be at!
I say no more than hath been said in Dante's
Verse, and by Solomon and by Cervantes;

By Swift, by Machiavel, by Rochefoucault,
  By Fénélon, by Luther, and by Plato;
By Tillotson, and Wesley, and Rousseau,
  Who knew this life was not worth a potato.
'T is not their fault, nor mine, if this be so, –
  For my part, I pretend not to be Cato,
Nor even Diogenes – We live and die,
But which is best, you know no more than I.

Socrates said, our only knowledge was
  'To know that nothing could be known;' a pleasant
Science enough, which levels to an ass
  Each man of wisdom, future, past, or present.
Newton (that proverb of the mind), alas!
  Declared, with all his grand discoveries recent,
That he himself felt only 'like a youth
Picking up shells by the great ocean – Truth.'

Ecclesiastes said, 'that all is vanity' –
    Most modern preachers say the same, or show it
By their examples of true Christianity:
    In short, all know, or very soon may know it;
And in this scene of all-confess'd inanity,
    By saint, by sage, by preacher and by poet,
Must I restrain me, through the fear of strife,
From holding up the nothingness of life?

Dogs, or men! – for I flatter you in saying
    That ye are dogs – your betters far – ye may
Read, or read not, what I am now essaying
    To show ye what ye are in every way.
As little as the moon stops for the baying
    Of wolves, will the bright Muse withdraw one ray
From out her skies – then howl your idle wrath!
While she still silvers o'er your gloomy path.

GEORGE GORDON, LORD BYRON

Public-House Confidence

Well, since you're from the other side of town,
I'll tell you how I hold a soft job down.
In the designing-rooms and laboratory
I'm dressed in overalls, and so pretend
To be on business from the factory.
The workmen think I'm from the other end.
The in-betweens and smart commission-men
Believe I must have some pull with the boss.
So, playing off the spanner against the pen,
I never let the rumour get across
Of how I am no use at all to either,
And draw the pay of both for doing neither.

NORMAN CAMERON

Bagpipe Music

It's no go the merrygoround, it's no go the rickshaw,
All we want is a limousine and a ticket for the peepshow.
Their knickers are made of crêpe-de-chine, their shoes are
  made of python,
Their halls are lined with tiger rugs and their walls with heads
  of bison.

John MacDonald found a corpse, put it under the sofa,
Waited till it came to life and hit it with a poker,
Sold its eyes for souvenirs, sold its blood for whiskey,
Kept its bones for dumb-bells to use when he was fifty.

It's no go the Yogi-Man, it's no go Blavatsky,
All we want is a bank balance and a bit of skirt in a taxi.

Annie MacDougall went to milk, caught her foot in the
  heather,
Woke to hear a dance record playing of Old Vienna.
It's no go your maidenheads, it's no go your culture,
All we want is a Dunlop tyre and the devil mend the puncture.

The Laird o' Phelps spent Hogmanay declaring he was sober,
Counted his feet to prove the fact and found he had one foot
  over.
Mrs Carmichael had her fifth, looked at the job with repulsion,
Said to the midwife 'Take it away; I'm through with over-
  production.'

It's no go the gossip column, it's no go the Ceilidh,
All we want is a mother's help and a sugar-stick for the
  baby.

Willie Murray cut his thumb, couldn't count the damage,
Took the hide of an Ayrshire cow and used it for a bandage.
His brother caught three hundred cran when the seas were
    lavish,
Threw the bleeders back in the sea and went upon the parish.

It's no go the Herring Board, it's no go the Bible,
All we want is a packet of fags when our hands are idle.

It's no go the picture palace, it's no go the stadium,
It's no go the country cot with a pot of pink geraniums,
It's no go the Government grants, it's no go the elections,
Sit on your arse for fifty years and hang your hat on a pension.

It's no go my honey love, it's no go my poppet;
Work your hands from day to day, the winds will blow the
    profit.
The glass is falling hour by hour, the glass will fall for ever,
But if you break the bloody glass you won't hold up the
    weather.

LOUIS MACNEICE

To Lar, with a Biscuit

There is no more
An Household God:
The Presiding Deities
Are gone,
Are sacked.

Love was all
They had for rod:
Not-loving all
They knew of wrong,
And thwacked.

No watch
Is on the household now!
Penates, Lares,
Emigrate,
Begone!

Daughters, sons,
Do anyhow:
And, as you please,
Perpetuate,
Each one,

The skunk, the badger,
And the cow!
– No altar's
In the household now,
No wit –

Only the monkey
And the sow
Tell what man should do,
And how
Do it.

JAMES STEPHENS

Anywhere Out of the World*

This life is an infirmary where each invalid is possessed by a desire to change beds. One man would sooner bear his pain in front of the stove, another man is certain he would recover over by the window. To me it seems I shall always be well in the place where I am not, and this question of moving is one I am always arguing with my soul.

'Tell me, my soul, my poor freezing soul, how would you like a move to Lisbon? It must be warm in Lisbon, it could make you spry as a lizard. That city stands on the edge of water: they say it is built of marble, they say the inhabitants detest the vegetal so much that every tree has been rooted up. That is your kind of landscape, a landscape compounded only of light and mineral, and liquid, which mirrors them!'

My soul makes no reply.

'Since you are so fond of repose, coupled with the spectacle of movement, would you like to go and live in Holland, that beatific land? Maybe you could find diversion in a country you have so often admired in picture galleries. In Rotterdam, do you think? You love masts crowded into a forest, and boats tied up under houses.'

My soul still says nothing.

'Maybe you would prefer Batavia? Where as well we should find the spirit of Europe allied with tropical beauty.'

Not a word. Could my soul be dead?

'Look, have you become so torpid that you don't care for

* Baudelaire's English title, from 'The Bridge of Sighs' by Thomas Hood:

> Mad from life's history,
> Glad to death's mystery,
> Swift to be hurl'd –
> Anywhere, anywhere,
> Out of the world!

CHARLES BAUDELAIRE · JAMES STEPHENS

anything any more but your own sickness? If that is it, let us
be off to those lands which are the analogues of Death. Poor
soul, I understand. We will pack our traps for Tornio. We
will go further on to the remotest end of the Baltic; further
still, if we can, away from life; we will set up house at the
Pole. There the sun only brushes the ground slantwise and the
slow alternatives of daylight and night suppress diversity and
augment monotony, that moiety of nothingness. There we
shall be able to take long baths of darkness, while, for our
diversion, the Northern Lights shall send us now and then
their rosy sheaves, like reflections of the firework shows of
Hell!'

At last my soul explodes, and screams to me in its wisdom
'Anywhere! anywhere! as long as it's out of this world!'

FROM THE PROSE POEMS OF CHARLES BAUDELAIRE
(*translated by Geoffrey Grigson*)

What's the Use

What's the use
Of my abuse?

The world will run
Around the sun

As it has done
Since time begun,

When I have drifted
To the deuce;

And what's the use
Of my abuse!

JAMES STEPHENS

195

Neither Sadness Nor Desire

Neither sadness nor desire
seems the edge: this precipice.

Delight dances,
everything works.

.

How wise age is –
How desirous!

.

Love's faint trace . . .

.

The smell of stale air
in this cramped room.
One sits. The shit falls
below the seat into water.

.

You have nor face nor hands
nor eyes nor head either.

. . .

ROBERT CREELEY

ABOUT THE RAFFISH

Adrian Mitchell's Famous Weak Bladder Blues

Now some praise God because he gave us the bomb to drop
    in 1945
But I thank the Lord for equipping me with the fastest cock
    alive.

You may think a sten-gun's frequent, you can call greased
    lightning fast,
But race them down to the Piccadilly bog and watch me
    zooming past.

  Well it's excuse me,
  And I'll be back.
  Door locked so rat-a-tat-tat.
  You mind if I go first?
  I'm holding this cloudburst.
  I'll be out in 3·7 seconds flat.

I've got the Adamant Trophy, the Niagara Cup, you should
    see me on the M.1 run,
For at every comfort station I've got a reputation for – doing
    the ton.

Once I met that Speedy Gonzales and he was first through the
    door.
But I was unzipped, let rip, zipped again and out before he
    could even draw.

Now God killed Vicky and he let Harold Wilson survive,
But the good Lord blessed little Adrian Mitchell with the
    fastest cock alive.

ADRIAN MITCHELL

199

The Complaint of the Fair Armouress

I

Meseemeth I heard cry and groan
   That sweet who was the armourer's maid;
For her young years she made sore moan,
   And right upon this wise she said;
   'Ah fierce old age with foul bald head,
To spoil fair things thou art over fain;
   Who holdeth me? who? would God I were dead!
Would God I were well dead and slain!

II

'Lo, thou hast broken the sweet yoke
   That my high beauty held above
All priests and clerks and merchant-folk;
   There was not one but for my love
   Would give me gold and gold enough,
Though sorrow his very heart had riven,
   To win from me such wage thereof
As now no thief would take if given.

III

'I was right chary of the same,
   God wot it was my great folly,
For love of one sly knave of them,
   Good store of that same sweet had he;
   For all my subtle wiles, perdie,
God wot I loved him well enow;
   Right evilly he handled me,
But he loved well my gold, I trow.

IV

'Though I gat bruises green and black,
　I loved him never the less a jot;
Though he bound burdens on my back,
　If he said "Kiss me and heed it not"
　Right little pain I felt, God wot,
When that foul thief's mouth, found so sweet,
　Kissed me – Much good thereof I got!
I keep the sin and the shame of it.

V

'And he died thirty year agone.
　I am old now, no sweet thing to see;
By God, though, when I think thereon,
　And of that good glad time, woe's me,
　And stare upon my changed body
Stark naked, that has been so sweet,
　Lean, wizen, like a small dry tree,
I am nigh mad with the pain of it.

VI

'Where is my faultless forehead's white,
　The lifted eyebrows, soft gold hair,
Eyes wide apart and keen of sight,
　With subtle skill in the amorous air;
　The straight nose, great nor small, but fair,
The small carved ears of shapeliest growth,
　Chin dimpling, colour good to wear,
And sweet red splendid kissing mouth?

VII

'The shapely slender shoulders small,
　Long arms, hands wrought in glorious wise,
Round little breasts, the hips withal
　High, full of flesh, not scant of size,

Fit for all amorous masteries;
The large loins, and the flower that was
  Planted above my strong, round thighs
In a small garden of soft grass?

VIII

'A writhled forehead, hair gone grey,
  Fallen eyebrows, eyes gone blind and red,
Their laughs and looks all fled away,
  Yea, all that smote men's hearts are fled;
  The bowed nose, fallen from goodlihead;
Foul flapping ears like water-flags;
  Peaked chin, and cheeks all waste and dead,
And lips that are two skinny rags:

IX

'Thus endeth all the beauty of us.
  The arms made short, the hands made lean,
The shoulders bowed and ruinous,
  The breasts, alack! all fallen in;
  The flanks too, like the breasts, grown thin;
As for the sweet place, out on it!
  For the lank thighs, no thighs but skin,
They are specked with spots like sausage-meat.

X

'So we make moan for the old sweet days,
  Poor old light women, two or three
Squatting above the straw-fire's blaze,
  The bosom crushed against the knee,

Like faggots on a heap we be,
Round fires soon lit, soon quenched and done;
    And we were once so sweet, even we!
Thus fareth many and many an one.'

FRANÇOIS VILLON
(*translated by A. C. Swinburne*)

Room, Room for a Blade of the Town

Room, Room for a Blade of the Town,
    That takes Delight in Roaring,
Who all Day long rambles up and down,
    And at Night in the Street lies Snoaring.

That for the Noble Name of Spark
    Does his Companions Rally;
Commits an Outrage in the Dark,
    Then slinks into an Alley.

To every Female that he meets,
    He swears he bears Affection,
Defies all Laws, Arrests, and Cheats,
    By the Help of a kind Protection.

When he intending further Wrongs,
    By some Resenting Cully
Is decently run through the Lungs
    And there's an end of BULLY.

THOMAS D'URFEY

The Ballad of Villon and Fat Madge

'''Tis no sin for a man to labour in his vocation.'
'The night cometh, when no man can work.'

What though the beauty I love and serve be cheap,
    Ought you to take me for a beast or fool?
All things a man could wish are in her keep;
    For her I turn swashbuckler in love's school.
    When folk drop in, I take my pot and stool
And fall to drinking with no more ado.
I fetch them bread, fruit, cheese, and water, too;
    I say all's right so long as I'm well paid;
'Look in again when your flesh troubles you,
    Inside this brothel where we drive our trade.'

But soon the devil's among us flesh and fell,
    When penniless to bed comes Madge my whore;
I loathe the very sight of her like hell.
    I snatch gown, girdle, surcoat, all she wore,
    And tell her, these shall stand against her score.
She grips her hips with both hands, cursing God,
Swearing by Jesus' body, bones, and blood,
    That they shall not. Then I, no whit dismayed,
Cross her cracked nose with some stray shiver of wood
    Inside this brothel where we drive our trade.

When all's up she drops me a windy word,
    Bloat like a beetle puffed and poisonous:
Grins, thumps my pate, and calls me dickey-bird,
    And cuffs me with a fist that's ponderous.
    We sleep like logs, being drunken both of us;
Then when we wake her womb begins to stir;

To save her seed she gets me under her
   Wheezing and whining, flat as planks are laid:
And thus she spoils me for a whoremonger
   Inside this brothel where we drive our trade.

Blow, hail or freeze, I've bread here baked rent free!
Whoring's my trade, and my whore pleases me;
   Bad cat, bad rat; we're just the same if weighed.
We that love filth, filth follows us, you see;
Honour flies from us, from her we flee
   Inside this brothel where we drive our trade.

FRANÇOIS VILLON
(*translated by A. C. Swinburne*)

A Glass of Beer

The lanky shank of a she in the inn over there
Nearly killed me for asking the loan of a glass of beer;
May the devil grip the whey-faced slut by the hair,
And beat bad manners out of her skin for a year.

That parboiled ape, with the toughest jaw you will see
On virtue's path, and a voice that would rasp the dead,
Came roaring and raging the minute she looked at me,
And threw me out of the house on the back of my head!

If I asked her master he'd give me a cask a day;
But she, with the beer at hand, not a gill would arrange!
May she marry a ghost and bear him a kitten, and may
The High King of Glory permit her to get the mange.

JAMES STEPHENS

The Joviall Crew

or

Beggars–Bush

In which a Mad Maunder doth vapour and swagger
With praiseing the Trade of a bonney bold Beggar.

A Beggar, a Beggar,
A Beggar I'le be,
There's none leads a Life so jocond as hee;
A Beggar I was,
And a Beggar I am,
A Beggar I'le be, from a Beggar I came:
If (as it begins) our Trading do fall,
I fear (at the last) we shall be Beggars all.
Our Tradesmen miscarry in all their affayrs
And few men grow wealthy, but Courtiers and Players.

A Craver my father,
A Maunder my mother,
A Filer my sister, a Filcher my brother,
A Canter my Unckle,
That cared not for Pelfe,
A Lifter my aunt, a Beggar myselfe.
In white wheaten straw, when their bellies were full,
Then I was begot, between Tinker and Trul.
And therefore a Beggar, a Beggar I'le be,
For none hath a spirit so jocond as he.

maunder beggar
craver one who craves, i.e. beggar
filer filer of gold and silver coins
canter rogue, i.e. speaker of cant, thieves' and beggars' language
lifter thief

When Boyes do come to us,
And that their intent is
To follow our Calling, we nere bind them Prentice,
Soon as they come too't,
We teach them to doo't,
And give them a Staff and a Wallet to boot.
We teach them their Lingua, to Crave and to Cant,
The devil is in them if then they can want.
If any are here that Beggars will bee,
We without Indentures will make them free.

We begg for our bread,
But sometimes it happens
We feast with Pigg, Pullet, Conny and Capons
For Churche's affairs
We are no Man-slayers
We have no religion, yet live by our prayers.
But if when we begg, Men will not draw their purses,
We charge and give fire, with a volley of curses,
The Devil confound your good Worship we cry,
And such a bold brazen fac'd Beggar am I.

ANONYMOUS

Blythsome Bridal

Fy let us a to the bridal,
For there will be lilting there,
For Jock's to be married to Maggie,
The lass wi the gowden hair.
And there will be langkail and porridge,
And bannocks of barley-meal,

langkail cabbage cooked with the leaves whole

And there will be good sawt herring,
  To relish a cogue of good ale.
    Fy let us, etc.

And there will be Sawney the soutar,
  And Will wi the meikle mou:
And there will be Tam the blutter,
  With Andrew the tinkler I trow;
And there will be bow'd-legged Robie,
  With thumbless Katie's goodman;
And there will be blue-cheeked Dowbie,
  And Lawrie the laird of the land.
    Fy let us, etc.

And there will be sowlibber Patie,
  And plucky-fac'd Wat i th' mill,
Capper-nos'd Francie, and Gibbie
  That wons in the how o the hill;
And there will be Alaster Sibbie,
  Wha in wi black Bessie did mool,
With snivling Lilly, and Tibby,
  The lass that stands oft on the stool.
    Fy let us, etc.

cogue wooden cup
soutar cobbler
blutter gabbler
sowlibber sow gelder
plucky pimply
capper copper
wons dwells
how hollow
mool make love
stool stool of repentance in the kirk

And Madge that was buckled to Stennie,
  And coft him grey breeks to his arse,
Wha after was hangit for stealing,
  Great mercy it happen'd nae warse;
And there will be gleed Georgy Janners,
  And Kirsh wi the lily-white leg,
Who gade to the south for manners,
  And bang'd up her wame in Mons Meg.
    Fy let us, etc.

And there will be Juden Maclourie,
  And blinkin daft Barbara Macleg,
Wi flea-lugged sharney-fac'd Lawrie,
  And shangy-mou'd halucket Meg,
And there will be happer-arsed Nansy,
  And fairy-fac'd Flowrie by name,
Muck Madie, and fat-hippet Grisy,
  The lass with the gowden wame.
    Fy let us, etc.

And there will be girn-again Gibby,
  Wi his glaiket wife Jenny Bell,
And measly-shin'd Mungo Macapie,
  The lad that was skipper himsel:

buckled married
coft bought
gleed squinting
wame belly
Mons Meg cannon at Edinburgh Castle
lugged eared
sharney-fac'd cowpat-faced
shangy-mou'd with a mouth like a cleft stick
halucket giddy
happer hopper
girn grin
glaiket flighty
measly-shin'd spotty-legged

There lads, and lasses in pearlings,
  Will feast i the heart of the ha,
On sybows, and risarts, and carlings,
  That are baith sodden and raw.
    Fy let us, etc.

And there will be fadges and brochen,
  With fouth of good gabbocks of skate,
Powsoudie, and drammock, and crowdie,
  And caller nowtfeet in a plate.
And there will be partens and buckies,
  And whytens and spaldings enew,
And singit sheepheads, and a haggies,
  And scadlips to sup till ye spue.
    Fy let us, etc.

pearlings lace-edged gowns
sybows chives
risarts radishes
carlings parched pease
sodden boiled
fadges rolls
brochen oatmeal with butter, honey and water
fouth plenty
gabbocks mouthfuls
powsoudie sheep's head soup
drammock, crowdie oatmeal and water
caller fresh
nowtfeet cow's feet
partens crabs
buckies whelks
whytens whitings
spaldings dried fish
scadlips hot barley broth (scald lips)

And there will be lapper'd-milk kebbucks,
  And sowens, and farles, and baps,
With swats, and well-scraped paunches,
  And brandy in stoups and in caps:
And there will be mealkail and castocks,
  And skink to sup till ye rive:
And roasts to roast on a brander
  Of flowks that were taken alive.
    Fy let us, etc.

Scrapt haddocks, wilks, dulse and tangles,
  And a mill of good snishing to prie;
When weary with eating, and drinking,
  We'll rise up and dance till we die.
    Then fy let us a to the bridal,
      For there will be lilting there,
    For Jock's to be married to Maggie,
      The lass wi the gowden hair.

ATTRIBUTED TO FRANCIS SEMPILL

lapper'd curdled
kebbucks cheeses
sowens fermented sour oatmeal
farles oatcakes
baps yeast rolls
swats small ale
caps drinking bowls
mealkail cabbage and oatmeal soup
castocks cabbage stalks
skink beef and vegetable soup
rive burst
brander gridiron
flowks flatfish
dulse edible seaweed
tangles another edible seaweed
snishing snuff
prie try

Villon's Straight Tip to All Cross Coves

Tout aux tavernes & aux filles

Suppose you screeve? or go cheap-jack?
  Or fake the broads? or fig a nag?
Or thimble-rig? or knap a yack?
  Or pitch a snide? or smash a rag?
  Suppose you duff? or nose and lag?
Or get the straight, and land your pot?
  How do you melt the multy swag?
Booze and the blowens cop the lot.

Fiddle, or fence, or mace, or mack,
  Or moskeneer, or flash the drag;
Dead-lurk a crib, or do a crack,
  Pad with a slang, or chuck a fag;
  Bonnet, or tout, or mump and gag;
Rattle the tats, or mark the spot:
  You cannot bag a single stag –
Booze and the blowens cop the lot.

Suppose you try a different tack,
  And on the square you flash your flag?
At penny-a-lining make your whack,
  Or with the mummers mump and gag?
  For nix, for nix the dibs you bag!
At any graft, no matter what,
  Your merry goblins soon stravag –
Booze and the blowens cop the lot.

ENVOY

It's up the spout and Charley Wag
With wipes and tickers and what not;
Until the squeezer nips your scrag,
Booze and the blowens cop the lot.

FRANÇOIS VILLON
(*translated by W. E. Henley*)

The English Wedding

Last Sunday I came – a man whom the Lord God made – to the town of Flint, with its great double walls and rounded bastions; may I see it all aflame! An obscure English wedding was there, with but little mead – an English feast! and I meant to earn a shining solid reward for my harper's art. So I began with ready speed, to sing an ode to the kinsmen; but all I got was mockery, spurning of my song, and grief. It was easy for hucksters of barley and corn to dismiss all my skill, and they laughed at my artistry, my well-prepared panegyric which they did not value; John of the Long Smock began to jabber of peas, and another about dung for his land. They all called for William the Piper to come to the table, a low fellow he must be. He came forward as though claiming his usual rights, though he did not look like a privileged man, with a groaning bag, a paunch of heavy guts, at the end of a stick between chest and arm. He rasped away, making startling grimaces, a horrid noise, from the swollen belly, bulging his eyes; he twisted his body here and there, and puffed his two cheeks out, playing with his fingers on a bell of hide – unsavoury conduct, fit for the unsavoury banqueters. He hunched his shoulders, amid the rout, under his cloak, like a worthless balladmonger; he snorted away, and bowed his head until it was on his breast, the very image of a kite with skilful zeal preening its feathers. The pigmy puffed, making an outlandish cry, blowing out the bag with a loud howl; it sang like the buzzing of a hornet, that devilish bag with the stick in its head, like a nightmare howl, fit to kill a mangy goose, like a sad bitch's hoarse howl in its hollow kennel; a harsh paunch with monotonous cry, throat-muscles squeezing out a song, with a neck like a crane's where he plays, like a stabbed goose screeching aloud. There are voices in that hollow bag like the ravings of a thousand cats: a monotonous, wounded, ailing, pregnant goat – no pay for its hire. After it ended its wheezing note, that cold songstress whom love would shun, Will got his fee, namely bean-soup and pennies (if they paid) and sometimes small halfpennies, not the largesse of a princely hand; while *I* was sent away in high vexation from the silly feast all empty-handed. I solemnly vow, I do forswear wretched Flint and all its children, and its wide, hellish furnace, and its English people and its piper! That they should be slaughtered is all my prayer, my curse in their midst and on their children; sure, if I go there again, may I never return alive!

FROM THE WELSH OF ?LEWIS GLYN COTHI OR TUDUR PENLLYN
(*translated by Kenneth Jackson*)

Gluttony the Deadly Sin

(from *The Vision of Piers Plowman*)

Now biginneth Gloton   for to go to shrifte,
And kaires him to-kirke-ward   his coupe to shewe.
Ac Beton the brewestere   bad him good morwe,
And asked of him with that   whiderward he wolde.
'To Holy Cherche,' quod he,   'for to here masse,

shrifte confession
kaires betakes
coupe sin
Beton the brewestere Betty the brewer

214

And sithen I wil be shriven,   and sinne no more.'
'I have good ale, gossip,' quod she,   'Gloten, wiltou assaye?'
'Hastou ought in thy purs   any hote spices?'
'I have peper and piones,' quod she,   'and a pound of garlik,
A ferthingworth of fenel-seed   for fasting-dayes.'
   Thanne goth Gloton in   and grete othes after.
Cesse the souteresse   sat on the benche,
Watt the warner   and his wyf bothe,
Timme the tinkere   and tweine of his prentis,
Hick the hakeneyman,   and Hugh the nedeler,
Clarice of Cockeslane,   and the clerk of the cherche,
Dawe the diker,   and a dozein other;
Sire Piers of Pridie,   and Pernel of Flaunders,
A ribibor, a ratoner,   a rakere of Chepe,
A ropere, a redingking,   and Rose the disheres,
Godfrey of Garlikhithe,   and Griffin the Walshe . . .
   There was laughing and louring   and 'Let go the cuppe,'
And seten so til evensong,   and songen umwhile,
Til Gloton had iglobbed   a galon and a gille.
His guttes gonne gothely   as two gredy sowes;

piones peonies, i.e. peony seeds
souteresse (female) cobbler
warner warrener (in charge of a rabbit warren)
hakeneyman horse hirer
nedeler needle maker
diker ditcher
ribibor rebeck player
ratoner rat catcher
rakere raker, street cleaner
ropere rope maker
redingking ? horse servant
disheres seller of dishes
Walshe Welshman
umwhile at times
iglobbed gulped down
gonne gothely began rumbling

215

He pissed a potel   in a Pater-noster-while,
And blew his rounde ruwet   at his rigge-bone ende,
That alle that herde that horn   held her nose after,
And wisheden it had be wexed   with a wisp of firses.
  He mighte neither steppe ne stonde   er he his staf hadde,
And thanne gan he go   liche a glemannes bicche,
Some time aside,   and some time arere,
As whoso leith lines   for to lacche foules.
And whan he drow to the dore,   thanne dimmed his eyen,
He stumbled on the threshewold   and threw to the erthe.
Clement the cobelere   caught him by the middel
For to lifte him aloft,   and leide him on his knees.
Ac Gloton was a gret cherl,   and a grim in the lifting,
And coughed up a caudel   in Clementes lappe:
Is none so hungry hound   in Hertfordshire
Durst lape of the levinges,   so unlovely they smaughte.
With al the wo of this world   his wyf and his wenche
Baren him home to his bed   and broughte him thereinne.
And after al this excess   he had an accidie,
That he sleep Saterday and Sonday   till sonne yede to reste.
Thanne waked he of his winking   and wiped his eyen;
The firste word that he warp   was, 'Where is the bolle?'

WILLIAM LANGLAND

potel two quarts
rounde ruwet round trumpet
rigge-bone ridge-bone, spine
wexed blocked
wisp of firses handful of gorse, furze
glemannes bicche (blind) singer's bitch
lacche catch
smaughte smacked
accidie lethargy, hang-over
winking dozing
warp uttered
bolle bowl

Air

(from *The Jolly Beggars*)

Tune: 'Jolly Mortals, fill your Glasses'

See the smoking bowl before us,
  Mark our jovial ragged ring!
Round and round take up the chorus,
  And in raptures let us sing –

> *Chorus*
> A fig for those by law protected!
>   Liberty's a glorious feast!
> Courts for cowards were erected,
>   Churches built to please the priest.

What is title, what is treasure,
  What is reputation's care?
If we lead a life of pleasure,
  'Tis no matter how or where!
      A fig for, etc.

With the ready trick and fable,
  Round we wander all the day;
And at night in barn or stable,
  Hug our doxies on the hay.
      A fig for, etc.

Does the train-attended carriage
  Thro' the country lighter rove?
Does the sober bed of marriage
  Witness brighter scenes of love?
      A fig for, etc.

Life is all a variorum,
  We regard not how it goes;
Let them cant about decorum,
  Who have character to lose.
      A fig for, etc.

Here's to budgets, bags and wallets!
  Here's to all the wandering train.
Here's our ragged brats and callets,
  One and all cry out, Amen!

            Chorus
    A fig for those by law protected!
      Liberty's a glorious feast!
    Courts for cowards were erected,
      Churches built to please the priest.

                      ROBERT BURNS

Thomas Logge

Here lies Thomas Logge – A Rascally Dogge;
  A poor useless creature – by choice as by nature;
Who never served God – for kindness or Rod;
Who, for pleasure or penny, – never did any
        Work in his life – but to marry a Wife,
          And live aye in strife:
        And all this he says – at the end of his days
          Lest some fine canting pen
          Should be at him again.

                      WALTER DE LA MARE

budgets pouches
callets trollops

218

from *The Drunkards Speech in a Mask*

Oh, what an Ebb of Drink have we?
  Bring, bring a Deluge, fill us up the Sea,
Let the vast Ocean be our mighty Cup:
We'll drink't, and all its Fishes too like Loaches up.
  Bid the *Canary* Fleet land here: we'll pay
    The Fraight, and Custom too defray:
Set every man a Ship, and when the Store
Is emptied; let them strait dispatch, and Sail for more:
    'Tis gone: and now have at the *Rhine*,
    With all its petty Rivulets of Wine:
The *Empire*'s Forces with the *Spanish* we'll combine,
We'll make their Drink too in confederacy joyn.
    'Ware *France* the next: this Round *Bordeaux* shall swallow,
Champagn, *Langon*, and *Burgundy* shall follow.
    Quick let's forestal *Lorain;*
We'll starve his Army, all their Quarters drain,
And without Treaty put an end to the Campagn.
Go, set the Universe a tilt, turn the Globe up,
  Squeeze out the last, the slow unwilling Drop:
A pox of empty Nature! since the World's drawn dry,
    'Tis time we quit mortality,
    'Tis time we now give out, and die,
Lest we are plagu'd with Dulness and Sobriety.
  Beset with Link-boys, we'll in triumph go,
A Troop of stagg'ring Ghosts down to the Shades below:
  Drunk we'll march off, and reel into the Tomb,
  Nature's convenient dark Retiring Room;
And there, from Noise remov'd, and all tumultuous strife,
Sleep out the dull Fatigue, and long Debauch of Life.

[*Tries to go off, but tumbles down, and falls asleep.*]

JOHN OLDHAM

The Hay Hotel

There is a window stuffed with hay
Like herbage in an oven cast;
And there we came at break of day
To soothe ourselves with light repast:
And men who worked before the mast
And drunken girls delectable:
A future symbol of our past
You'll, maybe, find the Hay Hotel.

Where are the great Kip Bullies gone,
The Bookies and outrageous Whores
Whom we so gaily rode upon
When youth was mine and youth was yours:
Tyrone Street of the crowded doors
And Faithful Place so infidel?
It matters little who explores
He'll only find the Hay Hotel.

Dick Lynam was a likely lad,
His back was straight; has he gone down?
And for a pal Jem Plant he had
Whose navel was like half a crown.
They were the talk of all Meck town;
And Norah Seymour loved them well;
Of all their haunts of lost renown
There's only left the Hay Hotel.

Fresh Nellie's gone and Mrs Mack,
May Oblong's gone and Number Five,
Where you could get so good a back
And drinks were so superlative;

Kip Bullies whoremasters in the Kips, the once licensed Red Light district in Dublin

Of all their nights, O Man Alive!
There is not left an oyster shell,
Where greens are gone the greys will thrive;
There's only left the Hay Hotel.

There's nothing left but ruin now
Where once the crazy cabfuls roared;
Where new-come sailors turned the prow
And Love-logged cattle-dealers snored:
The room where old Luke Irwin whored,
The stairs on which John Elwood fell:
Some things are better unencored:
There's only left the Hay Hotel.

Where is Piano Mary, say,
Who dwelt where Hell's Gates leave the street,
And all the tunes she used to play
Along your spine beneath the sheet?
She was a morsel passing sweet
And warmer than the gates of hell.
Who tunes her now between the feet?
Go ask them at the Hay Hotel.

L'ENVOI

Nay; never ask this week, fair Lord,
If, where they are now, all goes well,
So much depends on bed and board
They give them in the Hay Hotel.

OLIVER ST JOHN GOGARTY

The Lay of Oliver Gogarty

Come all ye bould Free Staters now and listen to my lay
And pay a close attention please to what I've got to say,
For 'tis the tale of a winter's night in last December drear
When Oliver St John Gogarty swam down the Salmon Weir.

As Oliver St John Gogarty one night sat in his home
A-writin' of prescriptions or composin' of a poem
Up rolled a gorgeous Rolls-Royce car and out a lady jumped
And at Oliver St John Gogarty's hall-door she loudly thumped.

'O! Oliver St John Gogarty,' said she, 'Now please come
    quick
For in a house some miles away a man lies mighty sick.'
Yet Oliver St John Gogarty to her made no reply,
But with a dextrous facial twist he gently closed one eye.

'O! Oliver St John Gogarty, come let yourself be led.'
Cried a couple of maskéd ruffians puttin' guns up to his
    head.
'I'm with you, boys,' cried he, 'but first, give me my big fur
    coat
And also let me have a scarf – my special care's the throat.'

They shoved him in the Rolls-Royce car and swiftly sped
    away,
What route they followed Oliver St John Gogarty can't
    say,
But they reached a house at Island Bridge and locked him in a
    room,
And said, 'Oliver St John Gogarty, prepare to meet your
    doom.'

Said he, 'Give me some minutes first to settle my affairs,
And let me have some moments' grace to say my last night's
    prayers.'
To this appeal his brutal guard was unable to say nay,
He was so amazed that Oliver St John Gogarty could pray.

Said Oliver St John Gogarty, 'My coat I beg you hold.'
The half-bewildered scoundrel then did as he was told.
Before he twigged what game was up, the coat was round his
    head
And Oliver St John Gogarty into the night had fled.

The rain came down like bullets, and the bullets fell like rain,
As Oliver St John Gogarty the river bank did gain,
He plunged into the ragin' tide and swum with courage bold,
Like brave Horatius long ago in the fabled days of old.

Then landin' he proceeded through the famous Phaynix Park,
The night was bitter cold and what was worse, extremely dark,
But Oliver St John Gogarty to this paid no regard,
Till he found himself a target for our gallant Civic Guard.

Cried Oliver St John Gogarty, 'A Senator am I,
The rebels I've tricked, the Liffey I've swum, and sorra the
    word's a lie.'
As they clad and fed that hero bold, said the sergeant with
    a wink,
'Faith, then, Oliver St John Gogarty, ye've too much bounce
    to sink.'

WILLIAM DAWSON

from *The Testament of Mr Andro Kennedy*

In die mee sepulture
    I will nane haif bot our awne gyng,
Et duos rusticos de rure
    Berand a berell on a styng;
Drynkand and playand cop out, evin,
    Sicut egomet solebam;
Singand and playand with hie stevin
    Potum meum cum fletu miscebam.

I will na preistis for me sing
    Dies illa, Dies ire;
Na yit na bellis for me ring,
    Sicut semper solet fieri;
Bot a bag pipe to play a spryng,
    Et unum ail wosp ante me
In stayd of baneris for to bring;
    Quatuor lagenas cervisie,

In die mee sepulture on the day of my burying
gyng gang
Et duos rusticos de rure and two rustics from the country
styng pole
cop out, evin ?cup empty at the same time
Sicut egomet solebam as I used to myself
stevin noise
Potum meum cum fletu miscebam I have mingled my drink with weeping
    (Vulgate Psalm CI)
Dies illa, Dies ire the medieval hymn *Dies Irae*, Day of Wrath, sung at
    burials
Sicut semper solet fieri as is always the rule
spryng a dance tune
Et unum ail wosp ante me And an ale bush (ale house sign) before me
baneris banners
Quatuor lagenas cervisie four flagons of beer

Within the graif to set sic thing
In modum crucis juxta me,
To fle the fendis, than hardely sing
De terra plasmasti me.

WILLIAM DUNBAR

My Epitaph

Here lies a bard, let epitaphs be true,
His vices many, and his virtues few;
Who always left religion in the lurch
But never left a tavern for a church,
Drank more from pewter than Pierian spring
And only in his cups was known to sing;
Laugh'd at the world, however it may blame,
And died regardless of his fate or fame.

H. J. DANIEL

Meum Est Propositum

Seething in my inmost guts with corrosive anger
I must now address my heart words of bitter rancour;
Being formed of air and froth, lacking stone and mortar,
I am like a leaf the winds toss to every quarter.

In modum crucis juxta me like a cross beside me
fle the fendis frighten off the fiends
than then
hardely bravely
De terra plasmasti me from the ground Thou hast fashioned me

Granted that a man of sense, set upon endurance,
Knows that building on a rock makes the best insurance,
Foolish fellow that I am, I am like a flowing
Stream that, ever changing place, knows not where it's going.

Like a ship without a crew drifting hither thither,
Like a bird on aery roads flying God knows whither,
Quite immune to lock and key, quite immune to fetters,
Craving for my kind I join troops of drunks and debtors.

Weighty principles, for me, are not worth my money,
What I love is light-o'-love, sweeter far than honey;
Let but Venus give commands, easy 'tis to follow,
Venus who eschews the heart that is cold and hollow.

Down the primrose path I trip, green and salad fashion,
Virtue mine anathema, vice my only passion;
Less in love with heavenly joys than with pleasures sinful,
Dead in soul I save my skin, grant it many a skinful.

Hard enough it is and more, looking at a virgin,
To control what wanton thoughts from one's nature burgeon;
Being young how can we heed such restrictive motions
When the sight of velvet skins fills us with emotions?

Gambling in my list of sins forms the second heading;
But when gambling leaves me stripped both of shirt and bed-
   ding,
Frozen though my flesh may be, in my mind I'm sweating,
Then it is that verse and song find their best begetting.

Third and last but far from least taverns must have mention
Which have never lacked, nor shall, most of my attention,

Till the holy angels come and my eyes discern 'em
Singing for the dead their long *requiem aeternam.*

My proposal is to die somewhere in a tavern,
Liquor near my dying lips gaping like a cavern;
Then will all the angels sing, in most joyful chorus:
'May the Lord look kindly on this old drunk before us!'

LOUIS MACNEICE
(*from the twelfth-century Latin of the 'Archipoeta'*)

Get Drunk

It is essential to be drunk all the time. That is all: there's no
other problem. If you do not want to feel the appalling weight
of Time which breaks your shoulders and bends you to the
ground, get drunk, and drunk again.

What with? Wine, poetry, or being good, please yourself.
But get drunk.

And if now and then, on the steps of a palace, on the green
grass of a ditch, in the glum loneliness of your room, you come
to, your drunken state abated or dissolved, ask the wind, ask
the wave, the star, the bird, the clock, ask all that runs away,
all that groans, all that wheels, all that sings, all that speaks,
what time it is; and the wind, the wave, the star, the bird, the
clock, will tell you: 'It is time to get drunk!' If you do not
want to be the martyred slaves of Time, get drunk, always get
drunk! With wine, with poetry or with being good. As you
please.

FROM THE PROSE POEMS OF CHARLES BAUDELAIRE
(*translated by Geoffrey Grigson*)

ABOUT VARIOUS SACRED COWS

Laying Down One's Life for the British Female
(from *The Bothie of Tober-na-Vuolich*)

Now supposing the French or the Neapolitan soldier
Should by some evil chance come exploring the Maison Serny
(Where the family English are all to assemble for safety),
Am I prepared to lay down my life for the British female?
Really, who knows? One has bowed and talked, till, little by
    little,
All the natural heat has escaped of the chivalrous spirit.
Oh, one conformed, of course; but one doesn't die for good
    manners,
Stab or shoot, or be shot, by way of a graceful attention.
No, if it should be at all, it should be on the barricades there;
Should I incarnadine ever this inky pacifical finger,
Sooner far should it be for this vapour of Italy's freedom,
Sooner far by the side of the d—d and dirty plebeians.
Ah, for a child in the street I could strike; for the full-blown
    lady –
Somehow, Eustace, alas! I have not felt the vocation.
Yet these people of course will expect, as of course, my pro-
    tection,
Vernon in radiant arms stand forth for the lovely Georgina,
And to appear, I suppose, were but common civility. Yes, and
Truly I do not desire they should either be killed or offended.
Oh, and of course you will say, 'When the time comes, you
    will be ready.'
Ah, but before it comes, am I to presume it will be so?
What I cannot feel now, am I to suppose that I shall feel?
Am I not free to attend for the ripe and indubious instinct?
Am I forbidden to wait for the clear and lawful perception?
Is it the calling of man to surrender his knowledge and insight

For the mere venture of what may, perhaps, be the virtuous
    action?
Must we, walking our earth, discerning a little, and hoping
Some plain visible task shall yet for our hands be assigned us, –
Must we abandon the future for fear of omitting the present,
Quit our own fireside hopes at the alien call of a neighbour,
To the mere possible shadow of Deity offer the victim?
And is all this, my friend, but a weak and ignoble refining,
Wholly unworthy the head or the heart of Your Own
    Correspondent?

ARTHUR HUGH CLOUGH

The Visit

(A Christmas Poem)

The Gingerbread House in the Gingerbread Forest,
    That's where it took place.
The gin, the St Vitus, the gingevitis,
    Whatever it was, her face

Was pinker than usual that night,
    Her lingerie more fluid,
While I, in the hopes of such delight,
    Had purchased of the Druid

A pair of plain brown envelopes
    In which there lay concealed
A certain ... But still wilder hopes
    Clamor to be revealed:

232

Grandmama in her thermal formal,
  Grandpapa in his cape,
Had just settled down to a less-than-normal
  Minuend of rape,

When out in the clutter of Forest Lawn
  Stone furniture there landed
A wee little ship, from whose wee little hatch
  There strode forth, openhanded,

A wee little man, with his little ol' eyes
  So shifty and lightnin'-quick
That we knew right away (oh, *what* a surprise!)
  That it *must* be Tricky-Dick.

We snuggled all close with the shivery sheets
  Pulled over our heads and then
We sprang into bed. The dirty old beast –
  No tellin' about some men –

He was coming *inside*. Where *else* could we hide?
  (Ooh, this was getting fun!)
He was trying the house for chimneys – no –
  And for doors – there was *only* one –

Oh goodie he found it. Around he bounded
  Casing the joint for Green,
Casing the joint for Red – confounded
  Snooper he was, and mean.

He knew what a stocking was used for: to hang.
  And goodies for kiddies: to hide.
To hide from the sniveling beggars. We sprang
  For the door. We had made it! Outside!

We twisted the key in the Gingerbread Lock
　In the Patented Blast-proof Door;
And that's where we've left him, the silly old crock.
　Merry Christmas, and Christmases more!

GEORGE STARBUCK

Worm Either Way

If you live along with all the other people
and are just like them, and conform, and are nice
you're just a worm –

and if you live with all the other people
and you don't like them and won't be like them and won't
　conform
then you're just the worm that has turned,
in either case, a worm.

The conforming worm stays just inside the skin
respectably unseen, and cheerfully gnaws away at the heart of
　life,
making it all rotten inside.

The unconforming worm – that is, the worm that has turned –
gnaws just the same, gnawing the substance out of life,
but he insists on gnawing a little hole in the social epidermis
and poking his head out and waving himself
and saying: Look at me, I am *not* respectable,
I do all the things the bourgeois daren't do,
I booze and fornicate and use foul language and despise your
　honest man. –

234

But why should the worm that has turned protest so much?
The bonnie bonnie bourgeois goes a-whoring up back streets
just the same.
The busy busy bourgeois imbibes his little share
just the same
if not more.
The pretty pretty bourgeois pinks his language just as pink
if not pinker,
and in private boasts his exploits even louder, if you ask me,
than the other.
While as to honesty, Oh look where the money lies!

So I can't see where the worm that has turned puts anything
    over
the worm that is too cunning to turn.
On the contrary, he merely gives himself away.
The turned worm shouts: I bravely booze!
the other says: Have one with me!
The turned worm boasts: I copulate!
the unturned says: You look it.
You're a d— b— b— p— bb—, says the worm that's turned.
Quite! says the other. Cuckoo!

D. H. LAWRENCE

(The child speaks)

Wretched woman that thou art
How thou piercest to my heart
With thy misery and graft
And thy lack of household craft.

LIGHTLY BOUND
(The mother answers)

You beastly child, I wish you had miscarried,
You beastly husband, I wish I had never married.
You hear the north wind riding fast past the window? He calls
    me.
Do you suppose I shall stay when I can go easily?

STEVIE SMITH

The Speculators

The night was stormy and dark,   The town was shut up in
sleep: Only those were abroad who were out on a lark,   Or
those who'd no beds to keep.

   I pass'd through the lonely street,   The wind did sing and
blow;   I could hear the policeman's feet   Clapping to and
fro.

   There stood a potato-man   In the midst of all the wet;   He
stood with his 'tato-can   In the lonely Haymarket.

   Two gents of dismal mien,   And dank and greasy rags,
Came out of a shop for gin,   Swaggering over the flags:

   Swaggering over the stones,   These shabby bucks did walk;
And I went and followed those seedy ones,   And listened to
their talk.

   Was I sober or awake?   Could I believe my ears?   Those
dismal beggars spake   Of nothing but railroad shares.

I wondered more and more: Says one – 'Good friend of mine, How many shares have you wrote for? In the Diddlesex Junction line?'

'I wrote for twenty,' says Jim, 'But they wouldn't give me one;' His comrade straight rebuked him For the folly he had done:

'O Jim, you are unawares Of the ways of this bad town; I always write for five hundred shares, And *then* they put me down.'

'And yet you got no shares,' Says Jim, 'for all your boast;' 'I *would* have wrote,' says Jack, 'but where Was the penny to pay the post?'

'I lost, for I couldn't pay That first instalment up; But here's taters smoking hot – I say Let's stop, my boy, and sup.'

And at this simple feast The while they did regale, I drew each ragged capitalist Down on my left thumb-nail.

Their talk did me perplex, All night I tumbled and tost, And thought of railroad specs., And how money was won and lost.

'Bless railroads everywhere,' I said, 'and the world's advance; Bless every railroad share In Italy, Ireland, France; For never a beggar need now despair, And every rogue has a chance.'

W. M. THACKERAY

If I had a rusty concrete mixer
I would fill it with Murcheson's Cough Elixir.
Doesn't the thought of it make you sick, sir?

ADRIAN MITCHELL

In Committee

As the committee musters,
'Silence for Noisy, let Noisy orate.'
Noisy himself blusters,
Shouldering up, mounting the dais,
And baritonely opens the debate
With cream-bun fallacies
With semi-nudes of platitudes
And testamentary feuds
Rushed at a slap-stick rate
To a jangling end.
Immediately he
Begins again, pleads confidentially:
'Be grateful to your Noisy,
The old firm, your old friend –'
Whose bagpipe lungs express
Emphatic tunelessness.
How could we draft a fair report
Till all old Noisy's variants have been aired,
His complimentary discords paired,
Bellowing and squealing sort by sort
In Noah's Ark fashion;
Noisy's actual invalidation?

Applause. Up jumps Hasty. 'Excellent Hasty,
Three cheers for Hasty,' sings out Hearty,

And is at once ejected
As he expected.
Hasty speaks. Hasty is diabetic,
Like a creature in spasms, pathetic, out of joint.
Stammers, cannot clear the point,
Only as he sinks back, from his seat
Spits out, 'Noisy you dog, you slug, you cheat.'
Enter the Chairman, late,
Gathers the threads of the debate,
Raps for order,
'Ragman, will you speak next, sir?'
Ragman pulls out his latest clippings,
Potsherds, tags of talk, flint chippings,
Quotations happy and miserable,
Various careless ologies, half a skull,
Commonplace books, blue books, cook books,
And artificial flies with tangled hooks.
'All genuine,' lamely says Ragman,
'Draw your own deductions, gentlemen,
I offer nothing.'

Critic crosses the floor, snuffling.
Draws casually from Ragman's bag
Two judgements, a fossil, a rag, a thread,
Compares them outspread,
'Here Noisy cheated, as Hasty said,
Though not as Hasty meant.
Use your discernment.
These objects prove both speakers lied:
One side first, then the other side.
  We can only say this much: –
So and So clearly is not such and such.
And the point is . . .' Critic wrinkles his nose.
'Use your discernment.'

Re-enter Hearty, enthusiastically repentant,
Cries 'Order, Order!' Uproar.
Chairman raps, is impotent.
Synthesis smoking in a corner
Groans, pulls himself together,
Holds his hand up, takes the floor,
'Gentleman, only a half-hour more
And nothing done. What's to be blamed?
No, no. Let us agree
First, that the motion's wrongly framed,
Two senses are confused, indeed three,
Next, the procedure's upside down.
Pray, Mr Chairman, Mr Secretary . . .
Let us hear Pro and Con
On the reconstituted motion.'

Pro and Con speak. Noisy makes no objection,
Busy recalling his oration
For instant publication.
Hasty makes no objection,
Busy clicking the blind cords up and down,
Nor Ragman (Ragman consults a Hebrew Lexicon),
Nor Critic (Critic drums with a pencil on the table),
Nor Hearty (Hearty is affable
In bubbling praise of Ragman's knowledge).
Synthesis sums up, nerves on edge.
Critic amends a small detail.
Synthesis accepts it, not too proud.
Chairman reads the draft-report aloud,
'Resolved that this day fortnight without fail . . .'

All vote, all approve
With show of brotherly love,
And the clock strikes, just in time.
Hearty proposes in pun-strewn rhyme

A vote of thanks to all the officers.
Cheers drown Hasty's angry bark.
Noisy begins: 'Gentlemen and Philosophers . . .'
Critic hums: 'Not too ill a morning's work.'
Ragman's on all fours after scraps and crumbs.
Chairman turns out the gas: 'Come, Ragman!' Ragman
    comes;
Synthesis left sitting in the dark:
'I shall resign tomorrow, why stay
Flattered as indispensable
By this old rabble,
Not indispensable: and going grey?'

ROBERT GRAVES

Sunny Prestatyn

Come To Sunny Prestatyn
Laughed the girl on the poster,
Kneeling up on the sand
In tautened white satin.
Behind her, a hunk of coast, a
Hotel with palms
Seemed to expand from her thighs and
Spread breast-lifting arms.

She was slapped up one day in March.
A couple of weeks, and her face
Was snaggle-toothed and boss-eyed;
Huge tits and a fissured crotch
Were scored well in, and the space
Between her legs held scrawls
That set her fairly astride
A tuberous cock and balls

Autographed *Titch Thomas*, while
Someone had used a knife
Or something to stab right through
The moustached lips of her smile.
She was too good for this life.
Very soon, a great transverse tear
Left only a hand and some blue.
Now *Fight Cancer* is there.

PHILIP LARKIN

True Democracy

I wish I was a gentleman
as full of wet as a watering-can
to pee in the eye of a police-man –

But my dear fellow, my dear fellow
can it be that you still don't know
that every man, whether high or low
is a gentleman if he thinks himself so? –

He is an' all, you bet 'e is!
I bet I am. – You can 'old yer phiz
abaht it. – Yes, I'm a gent, an' Liz
'ere, she's a lidy, aren't yer, old quizz? –

Of course I'm a lidy, what d'yer think?
You mind who yer sayin' isn't lidies!
All the hinglish is gentlemen an' lidies,
like the King an' Queen, though they're up just a wink –

– Of course you are, but let me say
I'm American, from New Orleans,
and in my country, just over the way,
we are *all* kings and queens! –

D. H. LAWRENCE

Democracy
(from *Les Illuminations*)

'The flag matches this filthy landscape, and our patois drowns the drum.

'We shall provision the most cynic prostitution in each centre. We shall massacre each inevitable uprising.

'Off to these sodden lands of pepper! – off to serve most monstrous exploitation by the military and merchant.

'So long, here, there, everywhere! We will live by the wisdom of beasts, conscripts because we want to be; know-nothings, lining our own nests; saying, World, piss off, go bust. That's the right route for us. So, forward! March!'

ARTHUR RIMBAUD
(translated by Geoffrey Grigson)

The Last Man

'Twas in the year two thousand and one,
A pleasant morning of May,
I sat on the gallows-tree all alone,
A chaunting a merry lay, –
To think how the pest had spared my life,
To sing with the larks that day!

When up the heath came a jolly knave,
Like a scarecrow, all in rags:
It made me crow to see his old duds
All abroad in the wind, like flags: –
So up he came to the timbers' foot
And pitch'd down his greasy bags. –

Good Lord! how blythe the old beggar was!
At pulling out his scraps, –
The very sight of his broken orts
Made a work in his wrinkled chaps:
'Come down,' says he, 'you Newgate bird,
And have a taste of my snaps!' –

Then down the rope, like a tar from the mast,
I slided, and by him stood;
But I wished myself on the gallows again
When I smelt that beggar's food,
A foul beef-bone and a mouldy crust;
'Oh!' quoth he, 'the heavens are good!'

Then after this grace he cast him down:
Says I, 'You'll get sweeter air
A pace or two off, on the windward side,'
For the felons' bones lay there.
But he only laugh'd at the empty skulls,
And offered them part of his fare.

'I never harm'd *them*, and they won't harm me:
Let the proud and the rich be cravens!'
I did not like that strange beggar man,
He look'd so up at the heavens.
Anon he shook out his empty old poke;
'There's the crumbs,' saith he, 'for the ravens!'

It made me angry to see his face,
It had such a jesting look;
But while I made up my mind to speak,
A small case-bottle he took:
Quoth he, 'though I gather the green water-cress,
My drink is not of the brook!'

Full manners-like he tender'd the dram;
Oh, it came of a dainty cask!
But, whenever it came to his turn to pull,
'Your leave, good sir, I must ask;
But I always wipe the brim with my sleeve,
When a hangman sups at my flask!'

And then he laugh'd so loudly and long,
The churl was quite out of breath;
I thought the very Old One was come
To mock me before my death,
And wish'd I had buried the dead men's bones
That were lying about the heath!

But the beggar gave me a jolly clap –
'Come, let us pledge each other,
For all the wide world is dead beside,
And we are brother and brother –
I've a yearning for thee in my heart,
As if we had come of one mother.

'I've a yearning for thee in my heart
That almost makes we weep,
For as I pass'd from town to town
The folks were all stone-asleep, –
But when I saw thee sitting aloft,
It made me both laugh and leap!'

Now a curse (I thought) be on his love,
And a curse upon his mirth, –
An' if it were not for that beggar man
I'd be the King of the earth, –
But I promis'd myself an hour should come
To make him rue his birth –

So down we sat and bous'd again
Till the sun was in mid-sky,
When, just when the gentle west wind came,
We hearken'd a dismal cry;
'Up, up, on the tree,' quoth the beggar man,
'Till these horrible dogs go by!'

And, lo! from the forest's far-off skirts,
They came all yelling for gore,
A hundred hounds pursuing at once,
And a panting hart before,
Till he sunk down at the gallows' foot,
And there his haunches they tore!

His haunches they tore, without a horn
To tell when the chase was done;
And there was not a single scarlet coat
To flaunt it in the sun! –
I turn'd, and look'd at the beggar man,
And his tears dropt one by one!

And with curses sore he chid at the hounds,
Till the last dropt out of sight,
Anon, saith he, 'Let's down again,
And ramble for our delight,
For the world's all free, and we may choose
A right cozie barn for tonight!'

246

With that, he set up his staff on end,
And it fell with the point due West;
So we far'd that way to a city great,
Where the folks had died of the pest –
It was fine to enter in house and hall
Wherever it liked me best;

For the porters all were stiff and cold,
And could not lift their heads;
And when we came where their masters lay,
The rats leapt out of the beds;
The grandest palaces in the land
Were as free as workhouse sheds.

But the beggar man made a mumping face,
And knocked at every gate:
It made me curse to hear how he whined,
So our fellowship turned to hate,
And I bade him walk the world by himself,
For I scorn'd so humble a mate!

So *he* turn'd right, and *I* turn'd left,
As if we had never met;
And I chose a fair stone house for myself,
For the city was all to let;
And for three brave holidays drank my fill
Of the choicest that I could get.

And because my jerkin was coarse and worn,
I got me a properer vest;
It was purple velvet, stitch'd o'er with gold,
And a shining star at the breast! –
'Twas enough to fetch old Joan from her grave
To see me so purely drest!

But Joan was dead and under the mould,
And every buxom lass;
In vain I watch'd, at the window pane
For a Christian soul to pass!
But sheep and kine wander'd up the street,
And browz'd on the new-come grass. –

When lo! I spied the old beggar man,
And lustily he did sing! –
His rags were lapp'd in a scarlet cloak,
And a crown he had like a King;
So he stept right up before my gate
And danc'd me a saucy fling!

Heaven mend us all! – but, within my mind,
I had killed him then and there;
To see him lording so braggart-like
That was born to his beggar's fare,
And how he had stolen the royal crown
His betters were meant to wear.

But God forbid that a thief should die
Without his share of the laws!
So I nimbly whipt my tackle out,
And soon tied up his claws, –
I was judge myself, and jury, and all,
And solemnly tried the cause.

But the beggar man would not plead, but cried
Like a babe without its corals,
For he knew how hard it is apt to go
When the law and a thief have quarrels, –
There was not a Christian soul alive
To speak a word for his morals.

Oh, how gaily I doff'd my costly gear,
And put on my work-day clothes;
I was tired of such a long Sunday life, –
And never was one of the sloths;
But the beggar man grumbled a weary deal,
And made many crooked mouths.

So I haul'd him off to the gallows' foot,
And blinded him in his bags;
'Twas a weary job to heave him up,
For a doom'd man always lags;
But by ten of the clock he was off his legs
In the wind, and airing his rags!

So there he hung, and there I stood,
The LAST MAN left alive,
To have my own will of all the earth:
 Quoth I, now I shall thrive!
But when was ever honey made
With one bee in a hive?

My conscience began to gnaw my heart,
Before the day was done,
For other men's lives had all gone out,
Like candles in the sun! –
But it seem'd as if I had broke, at last,
A thousand necks in one!

So I went and cut his body down
To bury it decentlie; –
God send there were any good soul alive
To do the like by me!
But the wild dogs came with terrible speed,
And bade me up the tree!

My sight was like a drunkard's sight,
And my head began to swim,
To see their jaws all white with foam,
Like the ravenous ocean brim; –
But when the wild dogs trotted away
Their jaws were bloody and grim!

Their jaws were bloody and grim, good Lord!
But the beggar man, where was he? –
There was naught of him but some ribbons of rags
Below the gallows' tree! –
I know the Devil, when I am dead,
Will send his hounds for me! –

I've buried my babies one by one,
And dug the deep hole for Joan,
And covered the faces of kith and kin,
And felt the old churchyard stone
Go cold to my heart, full many a time,
But I never felt so lone!

For the lion and Adam were company.
And the tiger him beguiled:
But the simple kine are foes to my life,
And the household brutes are wild.
If the veriest cur would lick my hand,
I could love it like a child!

And the beggar man's ghost besets my dream,
At night to make me madder, –
And my wretched conscience within my breast,
Is like a stinging adder; –
I sigh when I pass the gallows' foot,
And look at the rope and ladder! –

For hanging looks sweet, – but, alas! in vain
My desperate fancy begs, –
I must turn my cup of sorrows quite up,
And drink it to the dregs, –
For there is not another man alive,
In the world, to pull my legs!

THOMAS HOOD

Nottingham's New University

In Nottingham, that dismal town
where I went to school and college,
they've built a new university
for a new dispensation of knowledge.

Built it most grand and cakeily
out of the noble loot
derived from shrewd cash-chemistry
by good Sir Jesse Boot.

Little I thought, when I was a lad
and turned my modest penny
over on Boot's Cash Chemist's counter,
that Jesse, by turning many

millions of similar honest pence
over, would make a pile
that would rise at last and blossom out
in grand and cakey style

into a university
where smart men would dispense
doses of smart cash-chemistry
in language of common-sense!

251

That future Nottingham lads would be
cash-chemically B.Sc.
that Nottingham lights would rise and say:
– By Boots I am M.A.

From this I learn, though I knew it before
that culture has her roots
in the deep dung of cash, and lore
is a last offshoot of Boots.

D. H. LAWRENCE

The Stately with the Stinking
(from *Land of Empire*)

O Land of Empire, art and love!
   What is it that you show me?
A sky for Gods to tread above,
   A soil for pigs below me!
O in all place and shape and kind
   Beyond all thought and thinking,
The graceful with the gross combined,
   The stately with the stinking!
Whilst words of mighty love to trace,
   Which thy great walls I see on,
Thy porch I pace or take my place
   Within thee, great Pantheon,
What sights untold of contrast bold
   My ranging eyes must be on!
What though uprolled by young and old
   In slumbrous convolution
Neath pillared shade must lie displayed
   Bare limbs that scorn ablution,

Should husks that swine would never pick
   Bestrew that patterned paving,
And sores to make a surgeon sick
   For charity come craving?
Though oft the meditative cur
   Account it small intrusion
Through that great gate to quit the stir
   Of market-place confusion,
True brother of the bipeds there,
   If Nature's need requireth,
Lifts up his leg with tranquil air
   And tranquilly retireth:
Though priest think fit to stop and spit
   Beside the altar solemn,
Yet, boy, that nuisance why commit
   On this Corinthian column?

ARTHUR HUGH CLOUGH

A Veld Eclogue: The Pioneers

On the bare veld where nothing ever grows
Save beards and nails and blisters on the nose,
Johnny and Piet, two simple shepherds, lay
Watching their flock grow thinner every day –
Their one joint Nanny-goat, poor trustful thing,
That by the fence had waited since last spring
Lest any of the stakes that there were stuck
Should sprout a withered leaf for her to suck.
Rough was the labour of those hardy swains,
Sometimes they lay and waited for the rains,
Sometimes with busy twigs they switched the flies
Or paused to damn a passing nigger's eyes:

Sometimes, as now, they peeled them off their hose
And hacked the jiggers from their gnarly toes.
At times they lay and watched their blisters heal,
At others, sweated forth a scanty meal
Prone on their backs between their Nanny's shins –
After the manner of the Roman twins.
What wonder then, at such a flurry kept,
That sometimes – oftenest of all – they slept?
Yet for all that their simple hearts were gay,
And often would they trill the rustic lay,
For though the times were hard they could not bilk
Their brains of nonsense or their guts of milk;
And loud upon the hills with merry clang
The grand old saga of 'Ferreira' rang,
Till the baboons upon the topmost krans
Would leap for joy, career into a dance,
And all their Simian dignity forgot
Would hold a sort of Nagmaal on the spot,
Or, if to such comparisons we stoop –
A special rally of the Empire Group.
Think not that I on racial questions touch,
For one was Durban-born, the other Dutch.
I draw no line between them: for the two
Despise each other, and with reason too!
But, in this case, they both forgave the sin,
Each loved the other as a very twin –
One touch of tar-brush makes the whole world kin.
That they were true-bred children of the veld

jiggers subcutaneous parasites
Ferreira a smutty folk-song in Afrikaans
Nagmaal a reunion of South African peasants and their families for
purposes of social festivity, commerce and religious debauchery
Empire Group a society whose meetings are mentally and morally analo-
gous to the above

It could as easily be seen as smelt,
For clumsier horsemen never sat astride,
Worse shots about their hunting never lied –
Though Piet once laid a lioness out straight,
I must confess – through aiming at its mate;
And Johnny, though he stalked extremely well,
Even against the wind the game could smell:
Even a pole-cat wheezing with catarrh
Could have perceived his presence from afar.
One knew them at a glance for Pioneers
Though Piet, but two years since, had washed his ears:
Their musty jackets and moth-eaten hair
Showed them for children of the Open Air;
Besides red tufts, there shone upon their faces
That 'nameless something' which Bolitho traces
To gazing out across the 'open spaces',
As if the sharpest Taakhaar that he knows
Can see an inch beyond his own red nose,
As if the meanest cockney in existence
Can't see the sky at a far greater distance
With sun and moon and stars to blink his eyes on
Much farther off than any fenced horizon,
And Sirius and Aldebaran, forsooth,
As far away as he is from the truth.
But 'nameless somethings' and 'unbounded spaces'
Are still the heritage of 'younger races' –

Bolitho Hector, not William. Prolific and popular interpreter of the
'New Earth', the 'Open Spaces', etc., to which he even relates the
present writer's poems. Accounting for the mental and physical
'superiority' of the Colonial to the European, Bolitho writes – '"It's
the distance that does it," said my millionaire, looking at me with his
rather fine head chiselled on a background of cream madonna-lilies,
"it's the distance that does it."'

At least our novelists will have it so,
And, reader, who are we to tell them, 'No!'
We, who have never heard the 'call', or felt
The witching whatdyecallum of the veld?
As for that 'nameless something', it was there
Plain as the grime upon their ragged hair –
Bolitho calls it an 'inspired alertness'
And so it seemed (in spite of their inertness) –
A worried look, as if they half-expected
Something to happen, or half-recollected
Anything having happened there at all
Since old Oom Jaapie's heifer calved last fall.
As for the 'boundless spaces' – wild and free
They stretched around as far as eye could see,
Which, though not very far, was yet enough
To show a tree, four houses, and a bluff.
Geographers, who say the world's a sphere,
Are either ignorant, or mazed with beer,
Or liars – or have never read two pages
Of any of our novelists or sages
Who tell us plainly that the world's more wide
On the colonial than the other side,
That states and kingdoms are less vast and grand
Than ranches, farms and mealie-planted land,
And that wherever on the world's bald head
A province or protectorate is spread
The place straightway to vast proportions jumps
As with the goitre or a dose of mumps –
So that in shape our cosmos should compare
Less with an apple than a warty pear.
For all our scenery's in grander style
And there are far more furlongs to the mile
In Africa than Europe – though, no doubt
None but colonials have found this out.

For though our Drakenberg's most lofty scalps
Would scarcely reach the waist-line of the Alps,
Though Winterberg, beside the Pyrenees,
Would scarcely reach on tip-toe to their knees,
Nobody can deny that our hills rise
Far more majestically – for their size!
I mean that there is something grander, yes,
About the veld, than I can well express,
Something more vast – perhaps I don't mean that –
Something more round, and square, and steep, and flat –
No, well perhaps it's not quite that I mean
But something, rather, half-way in between,
Something more 'nameless' – That's the very word!
Something that can't be felt, or seen, or heard,
Or even thought – a kind of mental mist
That doesn't either matter or exist
But without which it would go very hard
With many a local novelist and bard –
Being the only trick they've ever done,
To bring in local colour where there's none;
And if I introduce the system too,
Blame only the traditions I pursue.
We left our shepherds in their open spaces
Sunning the 'nameless somethings' on their faces,
And also (but that's neither here nor there)
Scratching the 'nameless somethings' in their hair.
And there I'll leave them to complete my rhyme
In conversation learned and sublime:

PIET

That you're a poet, Johnny, you declare
Both in your verses and your length of hair,
And sure, why not? we've prophets in the land
Fit with the best of Israel's line to stand –

For Balaam's donkey only made him curse
But Totius' Ox inspired him into verse,
And I have often thought some work of note
Could well be written round our faithful goat;
The heroes of Thermopylae were writers
And sculptors too – in spite of being fighters –
The heroes of Bull-hoek and Bondleswaart
Should not be backward in the field of art.
Come – the Jew's-harp! – I'll thrum it while you sing,
Arise, and soar on music's golden wing!

JOHNNY

A simple goat was in her owners blest,
They milked her twice a day, then let her rest:
No wrangling rose between them – all was fair –
Which owned the head, or tail, they did not care:
Think not that I on racial questions touch
For one was British and the other Dutch.

So Johnny sang. His song was brief and true –
Had Creswell, Smuts or Hertzog half his nous,
There would be far more goats on the Karroo
And far less in the Senate and the House.

ROY CAMPBELL

Totius nom de plume of a popular Afrikaans bard. His masterpiece, *Die Os* (The Ox), is highly praised by Dr Hermann, the Cape Town Bergson, on account of the poet's having identified his mind and soul so completely with that of his subject. See *The Wayzgoose* (first page, with footnote).

'A clime so prosperous both to men and kine
That which were which a sage could scarce define.'

Bull Hoek (pron. *hook*) *and Bondleswaart* (i) shooting raid on unarmed religious sect; (ii) bombing raid, by air, on a village which complained at a dog-tax.

'next to of course god america i
love you land of the pilgrims' and so forth oh
say can you see by the dawn's early my
country 'tis of centuries come and go
and are no more what of it we should worry
in every language even deafanddumb
thy sons acclaim your glorious name by gorry
by jingo by gee by gosh by gum
why talk of beauty what could be more beaut-
iful than these heroic happy dead
who rushed like lions to the roaring slaughter
they did not stop to think they died instead
then shall the voice of liberty be mute?'

He spoke. And drank rapidly a glass of water

E. E. CUMMINGS

America

America I've given you all and now I'm nothing.
America two dollars and twentyseven cents January 17, 1956.
I can't stand on my own mind.
America when will we end the human war?
Go fuck yourself with your atom bomb.
I don't feel good don't bother me.
I won't write my poem till I'm in my right mind.
America when will you be angelic?
When will you take off your clothes?
When will you look at yourself through the grave?
When will you be worthy of your million Trotskyites?

America why are your libraries full of tears?

America when will you send your eggs to India?

I'm sick of your insane demands.

When can I go into the supermarket and buy what I need with my good looks?

America after all it is you and I who are perfect not the next world.

Your machinery is too much for me.

You made me want to be a saint.

There must be some other way to settle this argument.

Burroughs is in Tangiers I don't think he'll come back it's sinister.

Are you being sinister or is this some form of practical joke?

I'm trying to come to the point.

I refuse to give up my obsession.

America stop pushing I know what I'm doing.

America the plum blossoms are falling.

I haven't read the newspapers for months, everyday somebody goes on trial for murder.

America I feel sentimental about the Wobblies.

America I used to be a communist when I was a kid I'm not sorry.

I smoke marijuana every chance I get.

I sit in my house for days on end and stare at the roses in the closet.

When I go to Chinatown I get drunk and never get laid.

My mind is made up there's going to be trouble.

You should have seen me reading Marx.

My psychoanalyst thinks I'm perfectly right.

I won't say the Lord's Prayer.

I have mystical visions and cosmic vibrations.

America I still haven't told you what you did to Uncle Max after he came over from Russia.

I'm addressing you.

Are you going to let your emotional life be run by Time Magazine?

I'm obsessed by Time Magazine.

I read it every week.

Its cover stares at me every time I slink past the corner candy-store.

I read it in the basement of the Berkeley Public Library.

It's always telling me about responsibility. Businessmen are serious. Movie producers are serious. Everybody's serious but me.

It occurs to me that I am America.

I am talking to myself again.

Asia is rising against me.

I haven't got a chinaman's chance.

I'd better consider my national resources.

My national resources consist of two joints of marijuana millions of genitals an unpublished private literature that goes 1400 miles an hour and twentyfive-thousand mental institutions.

I say nothing about my prisons nor the millions of under-privileged who live in my flowerpots under the light of five hundred suns.

I have abolished the whorehouses of France, Tangiers is the next to go.

My ambition is to be President despite the fact that I'm a Catholic.

America how can I write a holy litany in your silly mood?

I will continue like Henry Ford my strophes are as individual as his automobiles more so they're all different sexes.

America I will sell you strophes $2500 apiece $500 down on your old strophe

America free Tom Mooney

America save the Spanish Loyalists
America Sacco & Vanzetti must not die
America I am the Scottsboro boys.
America when I was seven momma took me to Communist
    Cell meetings they sold us garbanzos a handful per ticket
    a ticket costs a nickel and the speeches were free everybody
    was angelic and sentimental about the workers it was all so
    sincere you have no idea what a good thing the party was
    in 1835 Scott Nearing was a grand old man a real mensch
    Mother Bloor made me cry I once saw Israel Amter plain.
    Everybody must have been a spy.
America you don't really want to go to war.
America it's them bad Russians.
Them Russians them Russians and them Chinamen. And them
    Russians.
The Russia wants to eat us alive. The Russia's power mad. She
    wants to take our cars from out our garages.
Her wants to grab Chicago. Her needs a Red Readers' Digest.
    Her wants our auto plants in Siberia. Him big bureaucracy
    running our fillingstations.
That no good. Ugh. Him make Indians learn read. Him need
    big black niggers. Hah. Her make us all work sixteen hours
    a day. Help.
America this is quite serious.
America this is the impression I get from looking in the tele-
    vision set.
America is this correct?
I'd better get right down to the job.
It's true I don't want to join the Army or turn lathes in
    precision parts factories, I'm nearsighted and psychopathic
    anyway.
America I'm putting my queer shoulder to the wheel.

ALLEN GINSBERG

Captain Carpenter

Captain Carpenter rose up in his prime
Put on his pistols and went riding out
But had got wellnigh nowhere at that time
Till he fell in with ladies in a rout.

It was a pretty lady and all her train
That played with him so sweetly but before
An hour she'd taken a sword with all her main
And twined him of his nose for evermore.

Captain Carpenter mounted up one day
And rode straightway into a stranger rogue
That looked unchristian but be that as may
The Captain did not wait upon prologue.

But drew upon him out of his great heart
The other swung against him with a club
And cracked his two legs at the shinny part
And let him roll and stick like any tub.

Captain Carpenter rode many a time
From male and female took he sundry harms
He met the wife of Satan crying 'I'm
The she-wolf bids you shall bear no more arms.'

Their strokes and counters whistled in the wind
I wish he had delivered half his blows
But where she should have made off like a hind
The bitch bit off his arms at the elbows.

And Captain Carpenter parted with his ears
To a black devil that used him in this wise
O Jesus ere his threescore and ten years
Another had plucked out his sweet blue eyes.

Captain Carpenter got up on his roan
And sallied from the gate in hell's despite
I heard him asking in the grimmest tone
If any enemy yet there was to fight?

'To any adversary it is fame
If he risk to be wounded by my tongue
Or burnt in two beneath my red heart's flame
Such are the perils he is cast among.

'But if he can he has a pretty choice
From an anatomy with little to lose
Whether he cut my tongue and take my voice
Or whether it be my round red heart he choose.'

It was the neatest knave that ever was seen
Stepping in perfume from his lady's bower
Who at this word put in his merry mien
And fell on Captain Carpenter like a tower.

I would not knock old fellows in the dust
But there lay Captain Carpenter on his back
His weapons were the old heart in his bust
And a blade shook between rotten teeth alack.

The rogue in scarlet and grey soon knew his mind
He wished to get his trophy and depart
With gentle apology and touch refined
He pierced him and produced the Captain's heart.

God's mercy rest on Captain Carpenter now
I thought him Sirs an honest gentleman
Citizen husband soldier and scholar enow
Let jangling kites eat of him if they can.

But God's deep curses follow after those
That shore him of his goodly nose and ears
His legs and strong arms at the two elbows
And eyes that had not watered seventy years.

The curse of hell upon the sleek upstart
That got the Captain finally on his back
And took the red red vitals of his heart
And made the kites to whet their beaks clack clack.

JOHN CROWE RANSOM

You cannot hope
    to bribe or twist,
thank God! the
    British journalist.

But, seeing what
    the man will do
unbribed, there's
    no occasion to.

HUMBERT WOLFE

Editor Whedon

To be able to see every side of every question;
To be on every side, to be everything, to be nothing long;
To pervert truth, to ride it for a purpose,
To use great feelings and passions of the human family
For base designs, for cunning ends,
To wear a mask like the Greek actors –
Your eight-page paper – behind which you huddle,
Bawling through the megaphone of big type:
'This is I, the giant.'
Thereby also living the life of a sneak-thief,
Poisoned with the anonymous words
Of your clandestine soul.
To scratch dirt over scandal for money,
And exhume it to the winds for revenge,
Or to sell papers,
Crushing reputations, or bodies, if need be,
To win at any cost, save your own life.
To glory in demoniac power, ditching civilization,
As a paranoiac boy puts a log on the track
And derails the express train.
To be an editor, as I was.
Then to lie here close by the river over the place
Where the sewage flows from the village,
And the empty cans and garbage are dumped,
And abortions are hidden.

EDGAR LEE MASTERS

EXASPERATION OVER LETTERS, ART, PUBLISHERS

The Albatross

Sometimes for sport the men of loafing crews
Snare the great albatrosses of the deep,
The indolent companions of their cruise
As through the bitter vastitudes they sweep.

Scarce have they fished aboard these airy kings
When helpless on such unaccustomed floors,
They piteously droop their huge white wings
And trail them at their sides like drifting oars.

How comical, how ugly, and how meek
Appears this soarer of celestial snows!
One, with his pipe, teases the golden beak,
One, limping, mocks the cripple as he goes.

The Poet, like this monarch of the clouds,
Despising archers, rides the storm elate.
But, stranded on the earth to jeering crowds,
The great wings of the giant baulk his gait.

CHARLES BAUDELAIRE
(*translated by Roy Campbell*)

Distribution of Honours for Literature

The grandest writer of late ages
Who wrapt up Rome in golden pages,
Whom scarcely Livius equal'd, Gibbon,
Died without star or cross or ribbon.

WALTER SAVAGE LANDOR

Dublin

(from *Elegy on the Archpoet William Butler Yeats Lately Dead*)

Sometimes you brought invective down
Upon the 'blind and ignorant town'
Which I would half disclaim;
For in my laughing heart I knew
Its scheming and demeaning crew
Was useful as the opposite to
The mood that leads to fame;
For very helpful is the town
Where we by contradicting come
Much nearer to our native home;
But yet it made me grieve
To think its mounted-beggar race
Makes Dublin the most famous place
For famous men to leave:
Where City Fathers staged a farce
And honoured one who owned a horse; ★
They win right well our sneers
Who of their son took no account
Though he had Pegasus to mount
And rode two hemispheres.
Return Dean Swift, and elevate
Our townsmen to the equine state!

OLIVER ST JOHN GOGARTY

★ Boss Croker, after his Tammany career, resided in Ireland and won the Derby with a horse bred in Ireland called Orby. The City Fathers gave Boss Croker the Freedom of the City but refused the author's suggestion that they give a similar honour to Yeats.

White Tom's Position

Tom, Tom, the pedants' father,
Master of perhaps, and rather.

Join your fingers, cross your knees,
Tell young poets to say please.

From your throne in Russell Square
Teach duchesses the art of prayer,

Teach the Tories to discount
Your master's Sermon on the Mount.

Teach the flaccid is the sound,
Proclaim the Pegasus of Pound.

Gird at Lawrence, Hardy, Blake,
For the Church of England's sake –

etc., and some day
  Over the Missouri, over the Seine,
    Over the Thames, and over the Severn,
  The soul of white Tom
    Shall float to Heaven.

ANONYMOUS

A Deep Amen

(from *One Way Song*)

You now solicit a few Enemy thrusts
At the stock poets' thickly bay-leaved busts.
Ranged in that portrait-place, of marble and clay,
August with the as-yet unwithered bay,
I seem to note a roman profile bland,
I hear the drone from out the cactus-land;
That must be the poet of the Hollow Men:
The lips seem bursting with a deep Amen.

WYNDHAM LEWIS

I.

LINES TO RALPH HODGSON ESQRE

How delightful to meet Mr Hodgson!
(Everyone wants to know *him*)
With his musical sound
And his Baskerville Hound
Which, just at a word from his master
Will follow you faster and faster
And tear you limb from limb.
How delightful to meet Mr Hodgson!
Who is worshipped by all waitresses
(They regard him as something apart)
While on his palate fine he presses
The juice of the gooseberry tart.
How delightful to meet Mr Hodgson!
    (Everyone wants to know *him*).

He has 999 canaries
And round his head finches and fairies
In jubilant rapture skim.
How delightful to meet Mr Hodgson!
   (Everyone wants to meet *him*).

2.

LINES FOR CUSCUSCARAWAY AND
MIRZA MURAD ALI BEG

How unpleasant to meet Mr Eliot!
With his features of clerical cut,
And his brow so grim
And his mouth so prim
And his conversation, so nicely
Restricted to What Precisely
And If and Perhaps and But.
How unpleasant to meet Mr Eliot!
With a bobtail cur
In a coat of fur
And a porpentine cat
And a wopsical hat:
How unpleasant to meet Mr Eliot!
   (Whether his mouth be open or shut).

T. S. ELIOT

Why Did I Write?

I

FROM *An Epistle from Mr Pope to Dr Arbuthnot*

Why did I write? what sin to me unknown
Dipt me in Ink, my Parents' or my own?
As yet a Child, nor yet a Fool to Fame,
I lisp'd in Numbers, for the Numbers came.
I left no Calling for this idle trade,
No Duty broke, no Father dis-obey'd.
The Muse but serv'd to ease some Friend, not Wife,
To help me thro' this long Disease, my Life.

2

FROM *First Satire of the Second Book of Horace Imitated*

I nod in Company, I wake at Night.
Fools rush into my Head, and so I write.

ALEXANDER POPE

When Klopstock England Defied

When Klopstock England defied,
Uprose William Blake in his pride;
For old Nobodaddy aloft
Farted & Belch'd & cough'd;
Then swore a great oath that made heaven quake,
And call'd aloud to English Blake.
Blake was giving his body ease
At Lambeth beneath the poplar trees.

From his seat then started he,
And turned him round three times three.
The Moon at that sight blush'd scarlet red,
The stars threw down their cups & fled,
And all the devils that were in hell
Answered with a ninefold yell.
Klopstock felt the intripled turn,
And all his bowels began to churn,
And his bowels turned round three times three,
And lock'd in his soul with a ninefold key,
That from his body it ne'er could be parted
Till to the last trumpet it was farted.
Then again old Nobodaddy swore
He ne'er had seen such a thing before,
Since Noah was shut in the ark,
Since Eve first chose her hellfire spark,
Since 'twas the fashion to go naked,
Since the old anything was created,
And so feeling, he beg'd me to turn again
And ease poor Klopstock's ninefold pain.
If Blake could do this when he rose up from a shite,
What might he not do if he sat down to write?

WILLIAM BLAKE

In my youth the growls.
In mine age the owls.
After death the ghouls.

ALFRED TENNYSON

The Man I Am

(from *One Way Song*)

I'm not the man that lifts the broad black hat.
I'm not the man's a *preux*, clichéed for chat.
I'm not the man that's sensitive to sex.
I'm not the fair Novello of the Waacs.
I'm not at breaking wind behind a hand
Too good. I'm not when hot the man that fanned
His cheek with a mouchoir. I'm not that kind.
I'm not a sot, but water leaves me blind,
I'm not too careful with a drop of Scotch,
I'm not particular about a blotch.
I'm not alert to spy out a blackhead,
I'm not the man that minds a dirty bed.
I'm not the man to ban a friend because
He breasts the brine in lousy bathing-drawers.
I'm not the guy to balk at a low smell,
I'm not the man to insist on asphodel.
This sounds like a He-fellow don't you think?
It sounds like that. I belch, I bawl, I drink.

The man I am to live and to let live.
The man I am to forget and to forgive.
The man I am to turn upon my heel
If neighbours crude hostility reveal.
The man I am to stand a world of pain.
The man I am to turn my back on gain.
The man I am somewhat to overdo
The man's part – to be simple, and brave and true.
The man I am to twist my coat about
A beggar in a cold wind. Clout for clout,

I am the man to part with more than most –
I am the perfect guest, the perfect host.
The man I am (don't take this for a boast)
To tread too softly, maybe, if I see
A dream's upon my neighbour's harsh tapis.
The man I am to exact what is due to men,
The man to exact it only with the pen –
The man I am to let the machete rust,
The man I am to cry – Dust to the dust!
'The Word commands our Flesh to Dust' – that's me!
I am the man to shun Hamlet's soliloquy.

WYNDHAM LEWIS

Some thirty inches from my nose
The frontier of my Person goes,
And all the untilled air between
Is private *pagus* or demesne.
Stranger, unless with bedroom eyes
I beckon you to fraternize,
Beware of rudely crossing it:
I have no gun, but I can spit.

W. H. AUDEN

The Laureate

Like a lizard in the sun, though not scuttling
When men approach, this wretch, this thing of rage,
Scowls and sits rhyming in his horny age.

His time and truth he has not bridged to ours,
But shrivelled by long heliotropic idling
He croaks at us his out-of-date humours.

Once long ago here was a poet; who died.
See how remorse twitching his mouth proclaims
It was no natural death, but suicide.

Arrogant, lean, unvenerable, he
Still turns for comfort to the western flames
That glitter a cold span above the sea.

ROBERT GRAVES

Southey Reaches Heaven

(from *A Vision of Judgement*)

The varlet was not an ill-favour'd knave;
   A good deal like a vulture in the face,
With a hook nose and a hawk's eye, which gave
   A smart and sharper-looking sort of grace
To his whole aspect, which, though rather grave,
   Was by no means so ugly as his case;
But that, indeed, was hopeless as can be.
Quite a poetic felony '*de se*'.

Then Michael blew his trump, and still'd the noise
   With one still greater, as is yet the mode
On earth besides; except some grumbling voice,
   Which now and then will make a slight inroad
Upon decorous silence, few will twice
   Lift up their lungs when fairly overcrow'd;
And now the bard could plead his own bad cause,
With all the attitudes of self-applause.

He said – (I only give the heads) – he said,
  He meant no harm in scribbling; 't was his way
Upon all topics; 't was, besides, his bread,
  Of which he butter'd both sides; 't would delay
Too long the assembly (he was pleased to dread),
  And take up rather more time than a day,
To name his works – he would but cite a few –
'Wat Tyler' – 'Rhymes on Blenheim' – 'Waterloo'.

He had written praises of a regicide;
  He had written praises of all kings what ever;
He had written for republics far and wide,
  And then against them bitterer than ever.
For pantisocracy he once had cried
  Aloud, a scheme less moral than 't was clever;
Then grew a hearty anti-jacobin –
Had turn'd his coat – and would have turn'd his skin.

He had sung against all battles, and again
  In their high praise and glory; he had call'd
Reviewing 'the ungentle craft', and then
  Become as base a critic as e'er crawl'd –
Fed, paid, and pamper'd by the very men
  By whom his muse and morals had been maul'd:
He had written much blank verse, and blanker prose,
And more of both than anybody knows.

He had written Wesley's life: – here turning round
  To Satan, 'Sir, I'm ready to write yours,
In two octavo volumes, nicely bound,
  With notes and preface, all that most allures
The pious purchaser; and there's no ground
  For fear, for I can choose my own reviewers:
So let me have the proper documents,
That I may add you to my other saints.'

Satan bow'd, and was silent. 'Well, if you,
   With amiable modesty, decline
My offer, what says Michael? There are few
   Whose memoirs could be render'd more divine.
Mine is a pen of all work; not so new
   As it was once, but I would make you shine
Like your own trumpet. By the way, my own
Has more of brass in it, and is as well blown.

'But talking about trumpets, here's my Vision!
   Now you shall judge, all people; yes, you shall
Judge with my judgement, and by my decision
   Be guided who shall enter heaven or fall.
I settle all these things by intuition,
   Times present, past, to come, heaven, hell, and all,
Like King Alfonso.   When I thus see double,
I save the Deity some worlds of trouble.'

He ceased, and drew forth an MS.; and no
   Persuasion on the part of devils, saints,
Or angels, now could stop the torrent; so
   He read the first three lines of the contents;
But at the fourth, the whole spiritual show
   Had vanish'd, with variety of scents,
Ambrosial and sulphureous, as they sprang,
Like lightning, off from his 'melodious twang'.

Those grand heroics acted as a spell:
   The angels stopp'd their ears and plied their pinions;
The devils ran howling, deafen'd, down to hell;
   The ghosts fled, gibbering, for their own dominions –
(For 't is not yet decided where they dwell,
   And I leave every man to his opinions);
Michael took refuge in his trump – but, lo!
His teeth were set on edge, he could not blow!

Saint Peter, who has hitherto been known
   For an impetuous saint, upraised his keys,
And at the fifth line knock'd the poet down;
   Who fell like Phaeton, but more at ease,
Into his lake, for there he did not drown;
   A different web being by the Destinies
Woven for the Laureate's final wreath, whene'er
Reform shall happen either here or there.

He first sank to the bottom – like his works,
   But soon rose to the surface – like himself;
For all corrupted things are buoy'd like corks,
   By their own rottenness, light as an elf,
Or wisp that flits o'er a morass: he lurks,
   It may be, still, like dull books on a shelf,
In his own den, to scrawl some 'Life' or 'Vision',
As Welborn says – 'the devil turn'd precisian'.

As for the rest, to come to the conclusion
   Of this true dream, the telescope is gone
Which kept my optics free from all delusion,
   And show'd me what I in my turn have shown;
All I saw farther, in the last confusion,
   Was that King George slipp'd into heaven for one;
And when the tumult dwindled to a calm,
I left him practising the hundredth psalm.

GEORGE GORDON, LORD BYRON

Wordsworth

Dank, limber verses, stuft with lakeside sedges,
And propt with rotten stakes from broken hedges.

WALTER SAVAGE LANDOR

Southey and Wordsworth

(from *Don Juan*)

I know that what our neighbours call '*longueurs*',
  (We've not so good a *word*, but have the *thing*,
In that complete perfection which insures
  An epic from Bob Southey every Spring –)
Form not the true temptation which allures
  The reader; but 't would not be hard to bring
Some fine examples of the *epopée*,
To prove its grand ingredient is *ennui*.

We learn from Horace, 'Homer sometimes sleeps';
  We feel without him, Wordsworth sometimes wakes, –
To show with what complacency he creeps,
  With his dear '*Waggoners*', around his lakes.
He wishes for 'a boat' to sail the deeps –
  Of ocean? – No, of air; and then he makes
Another outcry for 'a little boat',
And drivels seas to set it well afloat.

If he must fain sweep o'er the ethereal plain,
  And Pegasus runs restive in his 'Waggon',
Could he not beg the loan of Charles's Wain?
  Or pray Medea for a single dragon?

Or if, too classic for his vulgar brain,
   He fear'd his neck to venture such a nag on,
And he must needs mount nearer to the moon,
Could not the blockhead ask for a balloon?

'Pedlars', and 'Boats', and 'Waggons'! Oh! ye shades
   Of Pope and Dryden, are we come to this?
That trash of such sort not alone evades
   Contempt, but from the bathos' vast abyss
Floats scumlike uppermost, and these Jack Cades
   Of sense and song above your graves may hiss –
The 'little boatman' and his 'Peter Bell'
Can sneer at him who drew 'Achitophel'!

GEORGE GORDON, LORD BYRON

The Lost Leader*

I

Just for a handful of silver he left us,
   Just for a riband to stick in his coat –
Found the one gift of which fortune bereft us,
   Lost all the others she lets us devote;
They, with the gold to give, doled him out silver,
   So much was theirs who so little allowed:
How all our copper had gone for his service!
   Rags – were they purple, his heart had been proud!
We that had loved him so, followed him, honored him,
   Lived in his mild and magnificent eye,
Learned his great language, caught his clear accents,
   Made him our pattern to live and to die!
Shakespeare was of us, Milton was for us,

*Wordsworth in 1843 agrees to become Poet Laureate.

Burns, Shelley, were with us, – they watch from their
   graves!
He alone breaks from the van and the freemen,
  – He alone sinks to the rear and the slaves!

II

We shall march prospering – not through his presence;
   Songs may inspirit us, – not from his lyre;
Deeds will be done, – while he boasts his quiescence,
   Still bidding crouch whom the rest bade aspire:
Blot out his name, then, record one lost soul more,
   One task more declined, one more footpath untrod,
One more devils'-triumph and sorrow for angels,
   One wrong more to man, one more insult to God!
Life's night begins: let him never come back to us!
   There would be doubt, hesitation and pain,
Forced praise on our part – the glimmer of twilight,
   Never glad confident morning again!
Best fight on well, for we taught him – strike gallantly,
   Menace our heart ere we master his own;
Then let him receive the new knowledge and wait us,
   Pardoned in heaven, the first by the throne!

ROBERT BROWNING

To Evoke Posterity

To evoke posterity
Is to weep on your own grave,
Ventriloquizing for the unborn:
'Would you were present in flesh, hero!
What wreaths and junketings!'

And the punishment is fixed:
To be found fully ancestral,
To be cast in bronze for a city square,
To dribble green in times of rain
And stain the pedestal.

Spiders in the spread beard;
A life proverbial
On clergy lips a-cackle;
Eponymous institutes,
Their luckless architecture.

Two more dates of life and birth
For the hour of special study
From which all boys and girls of mettle
Twice a week play truant
And worn excuses try.

Alive, you have abhorred
The crowds on holiday
Jostling and whistling – yet would you air
Your death-mask, smoothly lidded,
Along the promenade?

ROBERT GRAVES

Fragment of a Character of Jacob Tonson, His Publisher

With leering Looks, Bull-fac'd, and freckl'd fair,
With two left Legs, and *Judas*-colour'd Hair,
And frowzy Pores that taint the ambient Air.

JOHN DRYDEN

To Mr Murray

Strahan, Tonson, Lintot of the times,
Patron and publisher of rhymes,
For thee the bard up Pindus climbs,
                My Murray.

To thee, with hope and terror dumb,
The unfledged MS. authors come;
Thou printest all – and sellest some –
                My Murray.

Upon thy table's baize so green
The last new Quarterly is seen, –
But where is thy new Magazine,
                My Murray?

Along thy sprucest bookshelves shine
The works thou deemest most divine –
The 'Art of Cookery', and mine,
                My Murray.

Tours, Travels, Essays, too, I wist,
And Sermons, to thy mill bring grist;
And then thou hast the 'Navy List',
                My Murray.

And Heaven forbid I should conclude
Without 'the Board of Longitude',
Although this narrow paper would,
                My Murray.

GEORGE GORDON, LORD BYRON

'let's start a magazine

to hell with literature
we want something redblooded

lousy with pure
reeking with stark
and fearlessly obscene

but really clean
get what I mean
let's not spoil it
let's make it serious

something authentic and delirious
you know something genuine like a mark
in a toilet

graced with guts and gutted
with grace'

squeeze your nuts and open your face

E. E. CUMMINGS

On Authors and Publishers

What Authors lose, their Booksellers have won,
So Pimps grow rich, while Gallants are undone.

ALEXANDER POPE

The Weavers

Many a time your father gave me aid
When I was down – and now I'm down again!
You mustn't take it bad, nor be dismayed
To know that youngsters ought to help old men,
And 'tis their duty to do that: Amen!

I have no cows, no sheep, no boots, no hat –
– The folk who gave me presents are all dead,
And all good luck died with them! Because of that
I won't pay what I owe you; but, instead,
I'll owe you till the dead rise from the dead.

You weave good shirts, and I weave, for my bread,
Good poetry – But you get paid at times!
The only rap I get is on my head:
But when it comes again that men like rhymes
– And pay for them – I'll pay you for your shirt!

JAMES STEPHENS

An Anthem

Lo the Bat with Leathern wing,
Winking & blinking,
Winking & blinking,
Winking & blinking,
Like Doctor Johnson.

'Oho', said Dr Johnson
To Scipio Africanus,
'If you don't own me a Philosopher,
'I'll kick your Roman Anus'.

'Aha', To Dr Johnson
Said Scipio Africanus,
'Lift up my Roman Petticoat
'And kiss my Roman Anus'.

And the Cellar goes down with a step.
  (Grand Chorus.)

WILLIAM BLAKE

When Sr Joshua Reynolds died
All Nature was degraded;
The King drop'd a tear into the Queen's Ear,
And all his Pictures Faded.

WILLIAM BLAKE

Limericks

ON THE PAINTER VAL PRINSEP

There is a creator called God
Whose creations are some of them odd.
  I maintain, and I shall,
  The creation of Val
Reflects little credit on God.

ON WHISTLER

There's a combative artist named Whistler
Who is, like his own hog's-hairs, a bristler:
   A tube of white lead
   And a punch on the head
Offer varied attractions to Whistler.

ON CHARLES AUGUSTUS HOWELL

There's a Portuguese person named Howell
Who lays on his lies with a trowel:
   Should he give over lying,
   'Twill be when he's dying,
For living is lying with Howell.

ON FREDERICK ELLIS

There is a publishing party named Ellis
Who's addicted to poets with bellies:
   He has at least two –
   One in fact, one in view –
And God knows what will happen to Ellis.

ON HIMSELF

There is a poor sneak called Rossetti;
As a painter with many kicks met he –
   With more as a man –
   But sometimes he ran,
And that saved the rear of Rossetti.

ON ROBERT BUCHANAN, WHO ATTACKED HIM UNDER THE PSEUDONYM OF 'THOMAS MAITLAND'

As a critic, the poet Buchanan
Thinks 'Pseudo' much safer than 'Anon'.
  Into Maitland he's shrunk,
  Yet the smell of the skunk
Guides the shuddering nose to Buchanan.

ON THE TWO AGNEWS

There are dealers in pictures named Agnew
Whose soft soap would make an old rag new:
  The Father of Lies
  With his tail to his eyes
Cries – 'Go it, Tom Agnew, Bill Agnew!'

D. G. ROSSETTI

The Poet Shadwell's Coronation

(from *Mac Flecknoe*)

Now Empress Fame had publisht the renown
Of *Shadwell's* Coronation through the Town.
Rows'd by report of Fame, the Nations meet,
From near *Bun-Hill* and distant *Watling-street.*
No Persian Carpets spread th'imperial way,
But scatter'd Limbs of mangled Poets lay;
From dusty shops neglected Authors come,
Martyrs of Pies and Reliques of the Bum.
Much *Heywood*, *Shirley*, *Ogleby* there lay,
But loads of *Shadwell* almost choakt the way.

Bilk't *Stationers* for Yeomen stood prepar'd
And *Herringman* was Captain of the Guard.
The hoary Prince in Majesty appear'd,
High on a Throne of his own Labours rear'd.
At his right hand our young *Ascanius* sat,
Rome's other hope and Pillar of the State.
His Brows thick fogs, instead of glories, grace,
And lambent dullness plaid around his face.

JOHN DRYDEN

Cibber

Cibber! write all thy Verses upon Glasses,
The only way to save 'em from our Arses.

ALEXANDER POPE

Now wits gain praise by copying other wits
As one Hog lives on what another shits.

ALEXANDER POPE

Fame's Farting Trumpet
Summons to the Throne of Dulness
(from *The Dunciad*)

And now had Fame's posterior Trumpet blown,
And all the Nations summon'd to the Throne.
The young, the old, who feel her inward sway,
One instinct seizes, and transports away.

None need a guide, by sure Attraction led,
And strong impulsive gravity of Head:
None want a place, for all their Centre found,
Hung to the Goddess, and coher'd around.
Not closer, orb in orb, conglob'd are seen
The buzzing Bees about their dusky Queen.

   The gath'ring number, as it moves along,
Involves a vast involuntary throng,
Who gently drawn, and struggling less and less,
Roll in her Vortex, and her pow'r confess.
Not those alone who passive own her laws,
But who, weak rebels, more advance her cause.
Whate'er of dunce in College or in Town
Sneers at another, in toupee or gown;
Whate'er of mungril no one class admits,
A wit with dunces, and a dunce with wits.

   Nor absent they, no members of her state,
Who pay her homage in her sons, the Great;
Who false to Phoebus, bow the knee to Baal;
Or impious, preach his Word without a call.
Patrons, who sneak from living worth to dead,
With-hold the pension, and set up the head;
Or vest dull Flatt'ry in the sacred Gown;
Or give from fool to fool the Laurel crown.
And (last and worst) with all the cant of wit,
Without the soul, the Muse's Hypocrit.

ALEXANDER POPE

The Critick Vermin

From hence the Critick Vermin sprung
With Harpy Claws, and Pois'nous Tongue,
Who fatten on poetick Scraps;
Too cunning to be caught in Trapps.
Dame Nature as the Learned show,
Provides each Animal it's Foe:
Hounds hunt the Hare, the wily Fox
Devours your Geese, the Wolf your Flocks:
Thus, Envy pleads a nat'ral Claim
To persecute the Muses Fame;
On Poets in all times abusive,
From *Homer* down to *Pope* inclusive.

Yet, what avails it to complain:
You try to take Revenge in vain.
A Rat your utmost Rage defyes
That safe behind the Wainscoat lyes.
Say, did you ever know by Sight
In Cheese an individual Mite?
Shew me the same numerick Flea,
That bit your Neck but Yesterday,
You then may boldly go in Quest
To find the Grub-Street Poet's Nest.
What Spunging-House in dread of Jayl
Receives them while they wait for Bayl?
What Ally are they nestled in,
To flourish o'er a Cup of Ginn?
Find the last Garrat where they lay,
Or Cellar, where they starve to Day.
Suppose you had them all trepann'd
With each a Libel in his Hand,

What Punishment would you inflict?
Or call 'em Rogues, or get 'em kickt:
These they have often try'd before;
You but oblige 'em so much more:
Themselves would be the first to tell,
To make their Trash the better sell.

    You have been Libell'd – Let us know
What senseless Cockscomb told you so,
Will you regard the Hawker's Cryes
Who in his Titles always lyes?
Whate'er the noisy Scoundrel says
It might be something in your Praise:
And, Praise bestow'd in Grub-Street Rimes,
Would vex one more a thousand Times.
'Till Block-heads blame, and Judges praise,
The Poet cannot claim his Bays;
On me, when Dunces are satyrick,
I take it for a Panegyrick.
Hated by Fools, and *Fools to hate*,
Be that my Motto, and my Fate.

JONATHAN SWIFT

Academic Graffiti

Henry Adams
Was mortally afraid of Madams:
In a disorderly house
He sat quiet as a mouse.

Mallarmé
Had too much to say:
He could never quite
Leave the paper white.

Thomas the Rhymer
Was probably a social climber:
He should have known Fairy Queens
Were beyond his means.

Paul Valéry
Earned a meagre salary
Walking through the Bois,
Observing his Moi.

W. H. AUDEN

Today's Poetry

Why do the Graces now desert the Muse?
They hate bright ribbons tying wooden shoes.

WALTER SAVAGE LANDOR

The New Timon, and the Poets

We know him, out of Shakespeare's art,
    And those fine curses which he spoke;
The old Timon, with his noble heart,
    That, strongly loathing, greatly broke.

296

So died the Old: here comes the New.
  Regard him: a familiar face:
I *thought* we knew him: What, it's you,
  The padded man – that wears the stays –

Who killed the girls and thrilled the boys,
  With dandy pathos when you wrote,
A Lion, you, that made a noise,
  And shook a mane en papillotes.

And once you tried the Muses too;
  You failed, Sir: therefore now you turn,
You fall on those who are to you,
  As Captain is to Subaltern.

But men of long-enduring hopes,
  And careless what this hour may bring,
Can pardon little would-be Popes
  And Brummels, when they try to sting.

An artist, Sir, should rest in Art,
  And waive a little of his claim;
To have the deep Poetic heart
  Is more than all poetic fame.

But you, Sir, you are hard to please;
  You never look but half content:
Nor like a gentleman at ease,
  With moral breadth of temperament.

And what with spites and what with fears,
  You cannot let a body be:
It's always ringing in your ears,
  'They call this man as good as *me*.'

What profits now to understand
  The merits of a spotless shirt –
A dapper boot – a little hand –
  If half the little soul is dirt?

You talk of tinsel! why we see
  The old mark of rouge upon your cheeks.
You prate of Nature! you are he
  That spilt his life about the cliques.

A Timon you! Nay, nay, for shame:
  It looks too arrogant a jest –
The fierce old man – to take *his* name
  You bandbox. Off, and let him rest.

ALFRED TENNYSON

Inscription for Shakespeare's Monument in Westminster Abbey

After an hundred and thirty years' nap,
Enter Shakespear, with a loud clap.

ALEXANDER POPE

Ringsend

(After Reading Tolstoy)

I will live in Ringsend
With a red-headed whore,
And the fan-light gone in
Where it lights the hall-door;

And listen each night
For her querulous shout,
As at last she streels in
And the pubs empty out.
To soothe that wild breast
With my old-fangled songs,
Till she feels it redressed
From inordinate wrongs,
Imagined, outrageous,
Preposterous wrongs,
Till peace at last comes,
Shall be all I will do,
Where the little lamp blooms
Like a rose in the stew;
And up the back-garden
The sound comes to me
Of the lapsing, unsoilable,
Whispering sea.

OLIVER ST JOHN GOGARTY

The Curse

To a sister of an enemy of the author's who disapproved of
'The Playboy'

Lord, confound this surly sister,
Blight her brow with blotch and blister,
Cramp her larynx, lung, and liver,
In her guts a galling give her.

299

Let her live to earn her dinners
In Mountjoy with seedy sinners:
Lord, this judgement quickly bring,
And I'm your servant, J. M. Synge.

J. M. SYNGE

Survey of Literature

In all the good Greek of Plato
I lack my roast beef and potato.

A better man was Aristotle,
Pulling steady on the bottle.

I dip my hat to Chaucer,
Swilling soup from his saucer,

And to Master Shakespeare
Who wrote big on small beer.

The abstemious Wordsworth
Subsisted on a curd's-worth,

But a slick one was Tennyson,
Putting gravy on his venison.

What these men had to eat and drink
Is what we say and what we think.

The influence of Milton
Came wry out of Stilton.

Sing a song for Percy Shelley,
Drowned in pale lemon jelly,

And for precious John Keats,
Dripping blood of pickled beets.

Then there was poor Willie Blake,
He foundered on sweet cake.

God have mercy on the sinner
Who must write with no dinner,

No gravy and no grub,
No pewter and no pub,

No belly and no bowels,
Only consonants and vowels.

JOHN CROWE RANSOM

Poetry

I, too, dislike it.
 Reading it, however, with a perfect contempt for it, one
                                                    discovers in
 it, after all, a place for the genuine.

MARIANNE MOORE

ON DEATH, IN ONE MOOD
AND ANOTHER

Some can gaze and not be sick,
But I could never learn the trick.
There's this to say for blood and breath,
They give a man a taste for death.

Captain Hall

My name is Captain Hall, Captain Hall, Captain Hall,
My name is Captain Hall, Captain Hall,
My name is Captain Hall and I only have one ball,
But it's better than none at all,
Damn your eyes, blast your soul,
But it's better than none at all, damn your eyes.

They say I killed a man, killed a man,
They say I killed a man, killed a man,
I hit him on the head with a bloody lump of lead,
And now the fellow's dead,
Damn his eyes, blast his soul,
And now the fellow's dead, damn his eyes.

And now I'm in a cell, in a cell, in a cell,
And now I'm in a cell, in a cell,
And now I'm in a cell and on my way to hell,
Perhaps it's just as well,
Damn your eyes, blast your soul,
Perhaps it's just as well, damn your eyes.

The Chaplain he will come, he will come, he will come,
The Chaplain he will come, he will come,
The Chaplain he will come and he'll look so bloomin' glum,
As he talks of Kingdom come,
Damn his eyes, blast his soul,
As he talks of Kingdom come, damn his eyes.

Now this is my last knell, my last knell, my last knell,
Now this is my last knell, my last knell,
Now this is my last knell, and you've had a sell,
For I'll meet you all in hell,
Damn your eyes, blast your soul,
For I'll meet you all in hell, damn your eyes.

Now I feel the rope, feel the rope, feel the rope,
Now I feel the rope, feel the rope,
Now I feel the rope, and I've lost all earthly hope,
Nothing but the Chaplain's soap,
Damn his eyes, blast his soul,
Nothing but the Chaplain's soap, damn his eyes.

Now I am in hell, am in hell, am in hell,
Now I am in hell, am in hell.
Now I am in hell, and it's such a sell
Because the Chaplain's here as well,
Damn his eyes, blast his soul,
Because the Chaplain's here as well, damn his eyes.

ANONYMOUS

Epitaph on John Hewet and Sarah Drew in the Churchyard at Stanton Harcourt

NEAR THIS PLACE LIE THE BODIES OF
JOHN HEWET AND SARAH DREW
AN INDUSTRIOUS YOUNG MAN, AND
VIRTUOUS MAIDEN OF THIS PARISH;
CONTRACTED IN MARRIAGE
WHO BEING WITH MANY OTHERS AT HARVEST
WORK, WERE BOTH IN AN INSTANT KILLED
BY LIGHTNING ON THE LAST DAY OF JULY
1718

Think not by rigorous judgement seiz'd,
   A pair so faithful could expire;
Victims so pure Heav'n saw well pleas'd
   And snatch'd them in Cœlestial fire.

Live well and fear no sudden fate;
   When God calls Virtue to the grave,
Alike tis Justice, soon or late,
   Mercy alike to kill or save.

Virtue unmov'd can hear the Call,
And face the Flash that melts the Ball.

EPITAPH ON THE STANTON HARCOURT LOVERS

Here lye two poor Lovers, who had the mishap
Tho very chaste people, to die of a Clap.

ALEXANDER POPE

A Visit to the Dead

I bought (I was too wealthy for my age)
A passage to the dead ones' habitat,
And learnt, under their tutelage,
To twitter like a bat

In imitation of their dialect.
Crudely I aped their subtle practices;
By instinct knew how to respect
Their strict observances.

The regions of the dead are small and pent,
Their movements faint, sparing of energy.
Yet, like an exiled Government,
With so much jealousy

As were the issue a campaign or Crown,
They hold debates, wage Cabinet intrigues,
Move token forces up and down,
Turn inches into leagues.

Long I was caught up in their twilit strife.
Almost they got me, almost had me weaned
From all my memory of life.
But laughter supervened:

Laughter, like sunlight in the cucumber,
The innermost resource, that does not fail.
I, Marco Polo, traveller,
Am back, with what a tale!

NORMAN CAMERON

Quatrain Made When He Was Condemned to the Gallows *

François. A Frenchman. Birthplace, bloody old
Paris-by-Pontoise. That's me, that weights my days,
On two yards' rope this neck of mine
Will know now what my backside weighs.

FRANÇOIS VILLON
(translated by Geoffrey Grigson)

Charon

The conductor's hands were black with money:
Hold on to your ticket, he said, the inspector's
Mind is black with suspicion, and hold on to
That dissolving map. We moved through London,
We could see the pigeons through the glass but failed
To hear their rumours of wars, we could see
The lost dog barking but never knew
That his bark was as shrill as a cock crowing,
We just jogged on, at each request
Stop there was a crowd of aggressively vacant
Faces, we just jogged on, eternity
Gave itself airs in revolving lights
And then we came to the Thames and all
The bridges were down, the further shore
Was lost in fog, so we asked the conductor
What we should do. He said: Take the ferry
Faute de mieux. We flicked the flashlight

---

* As a Parisian, under French jurisdiction.

And there was the ferryman just as Virgil
And Dante had seen him. He looked at us coldly
And his eyes were dead and his hands on the oar
Were black with obols and varicose veins
Marbled his calves and he said to us coldly:
If you want to die you will have to pay for it.

LOUIS MACNEICE

Bog-Face

Dear little Bog-Face,
Why are you so cold?
And why do you lie with your eyes shut? –
You are not very old.

I am a Child of this World,
And a Child of Grace,
And Mother, I shall be glad when it is over,
I am Bog-Face.

STEVIE SMITH

Before Life and After

A time there was – as one may guess
And as, indeed, earth's testimonies tell –
  Before the birth of consciousness,
      When all went well.

None suffered sickness, love, or loss,
None knew regret, starved hope, or heart-burnings;
    None cared whatever crash or cross
        Brought wrack to things.

If something ceased, no tongue bewailed,
If something winced and waned, no heart was wrung;
    If brightness dimmed, and dark prevailed,
        No sense was stung.

But the disease of feeling germed,
And primal rightness took the tinct of wrong;
    Ere nescience shall be reaffirmed
        How long, how long?

THOMAS HARDY

The Epitaph in Form of a Ballad

(Which Villon made for himself and his comrades, expecting to
be hanged along with them)

Men, brother men, that after us yet live,
    Let not your hearts too hard against us be;
For if some pity of us poor men ye give,
    The sooner God shall take of you pity.
    Here are we five or six strung up, you see,
And here the flesh that all too well we fed
Bit by bit eaten and rotten, rent and shred,
    And we the bones grow dust and ash withal;
Let no man laugh at us discomforted,
    But pray to God that he forgive us all.

311

If we call on you, brothers, to forgive,
  Ye should not hold our prayer in scorn, though we
Were slain by law; ye know that all alive
  Have not wit alway to walk righteously;
  Make therefore intercession heartily
With him that of a virgin's womb was bred,
That his grace be not as a dry well-head
  For us, nor let hell's thunder on us fall;
We are dead, let no man harry or vex us dead,
  But pray to God that he forgive us all.

The rain has washed and laundered us all five,
  And the sun dried and blackened; yea, perdie,
Ravens and pies with beaks that rend and rive
  Have dug our eyes out, and plucked off for fee
  Our beards and eyebrows; never are we free,
Not once, to rest; but here and there still sped,
Drive at its wild will by the wind's change led,
  More pecked of birds than fruits on garden-wall;
Men, for God's love, let no gibe here be said,
  But pray to God that he forgive us all.

Prince Jesus, that of all art lord and head,
Keep us, that hell be not our bitter bed;
  We have nought to do in such a master's hall.
Be not ye therefore of our fellowhead,
  But pray to God that he forgive us all.

FRANÇOIS VILLON
(translated by A. C. Swinburne)

Rifle-Range and Cemetery

Café, with View of the Cemetery. – 'Strange notice,' our rambler says to himself, 'but calculated to make one thirsty! Certainly the proprietor of this establishment knows how to appreciate Horace and those poets who are followers of Epicurus. He may even be acquainted with that subtle profundity of the old Egyptians for whom there could be no good feast without a skeleton, or without some emblem of the brevity of life.'

And he went in, drank a glass of beer looking out on to the gravestones, and slowly smoked a cigar. Then he fancied going down into the cemetery, where the grass was so high and so inviting, and where the sun reigned with such splendour.

Yes, there was a fury of light and heat down there, and one could have said that the sun was drunk and wallowed at full length on a carpet of magnificent flowers manured by dissolution. An immense murmuration of life filled the air – the life of all things infinitesimal – broken at regular intervals by cracklings of fire from a neighbouring rifle-range, which burst like champagne corks exploding in the hum of a muted symphony.

Then, under the sun which heated his brain and in the atmosphere of the ardent perfumes of Death, he heard a voice whisper under the tomb he sat on. And this voice was saying: 'A curse on your butts and your rifles, you restless living, who bother so little for the dead and their divine repose! A curse on your ambitions, a curse on your calculations, impatient mortals, who come to study the art of killing alongside the sanctuary of Death! If you understood how easy that prize is to win, how easy it is to hit that target, and how all things

save Death are nothing, you would not tire yourselves so
much, industrious creatures, and you would trouble less often
the sleep of those who have so long achieved the Target, the
one true target of the hatefulness of life.'

FROM THE PROSE POEMS OF CHARLES BAUDELAIRE
(*translated by Geoffrey Grigson*)

To The Postboy

ROCHESTER: Son of a whore, God damn you! can you tell
A peerless peer the readiest way to Hell?
I've outswilled Bacchus, sworn of my own make
Oaths would fright Furies, and make Pluto quake;
I've swived more whores more ways than Sodom's walls
E'er knew, or the College of Rome's Cardinals.
Witness heroic scars – Look here, ne'er go! –
Cerecloths and ulcers from the top to toe!
Frighted at my own mischiefs, I have fled
And bravely left my life's defender dead;
Broke houses to break chastity, and dyed
That floor with murder which my lust denied.
Pox on 't, why do I speak of these poor things?
I have blasphemed my God, and libeled Kings!
The readiest way to Hell – Come, quick!
BOY: Ne'er stir:
The readiest way, my Lord, 's by Rochester.

JOHN WILMOT, EARL OF ROCHESTER

Grizzel Grimme

Here lies with Death auld Grizzel Grimme,
  Lincluden's ugly witch;
O Death, how horrid is thy taste
  To lie with such a bitch!

ANONYMOUS

INDEXES

Index of Titles and First Lines

Note: titles are given in *italics*.

Index of Poets and Translators